BECOMING A LIVING TESTIMONY

My journey through kidney disease and how it blessed my life

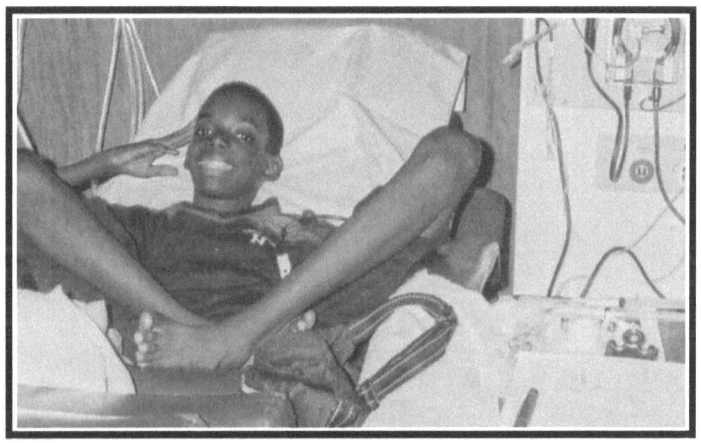

A MEMOIR BY:
ARTavius Veasey

FORWARD BY
DAPHAROAH69

ARTavius Veasey

"Becoming A Living Testimony" COPYRIGHT © BY: Artavius Veasey. Written by Artavius Veasey. ALL RIGHTS RESERVED by the Author.

LIBRARY OF CONGRESS CATALOGING-IN-PUBLICATION DATA HAS BEEN APPLIED FOR.

Editing and Interior Design by Larry Wilson, Jr., Dapharoah69: The King of Σrotica®

BECOMING A LIVING TESTIMONY

WITHOUT LIMITING THE RIGHTS UNDER COPYRIGHT RESERVED ABOVE, NO PART OF THIS PUBLICATION MAY BE REPRODUCED, STORED IN OR INTRODUCED INTO A RETRIEVAL SYSTEM, OR TRANSMITTED, IN ANY FORM, OR BY ANY MEANS (ELECTRONIC, MECHANICAL, PHOTOCOPYING, RECORDING, OR OTHERWISE), WITHOUT THE PRIOR WRITTEN AND SIGNED PERMISSION OF THE COPYRIGHT OWNER AND THE ABOVE PUBLISHER OF THIS BOOK, ARTAVIUS VEASEY.

DEDICATION:

For my first book, a memoir, I would love to dedicate it to my family.

My parents:
Tremetrius Barnes and Archie Veasey.

Without you two I wouldn't be here. Even though our relationship wasn't the best at times, when I needed either of you, you were always there. I couldn't be more thankful for that. Thank you!

My Grandmother:
Shirley Veasey. (Gma Shirley)

I don't know where to start. Thank you. You have been my guardian angel. You've given me your last so I can have. You're such a loving, nurturing, providing and God-fearing woman. I aspire to be just like you as I inevitably evolve into whom I'm destined to be. You've treated me as if I was your child. In my life it feels as if you are my mother. Thank you for everything you've done for me. I can honestly say I'm the man that I am today because of you and I'm forever grateful for that.

My Aunt:
Wanda Veasey. (TT Wanda).

You've been my best friend and biggest supporter in everything I do. I can't thank you enough for all the love and support you've shown me my entire life. Thank you for everything. Love You!

My Siblings:
Ashley, Reginald, Danisha, Terrance and Shirilyn.

All of them, my siblings, have become my biggest motivators. They are the reasons why I work as hard as I do. As the oldest sibling, I believe it's my duty and my right to lay the foundation for my family's future. I would never want them to go through the things that I've struggled with, but I know that I don't have control over that. However, I can do my absolute best to guide my siblings the best way I know how. I love each of them so much. They know that I support them in whatever they do. My wish is for all of them to achieve and accomplish everything their hearts desire, plus some. I want them to be bigger and greater than I am. Most importantly, I want each of my siblings, friends and family members to be happy. No matter what it is in life that they want to do or be, if it makes them happy, DO IT!

    I am so proud to be able to sit and watch my siblings become young, successful, classy adults. Even though we were all raised in different households and rarely got to see each other, I want them to know the love was and will forever be there. To my brothers and sisters, if you ever need me, you know my number and I'll come running from wherever I may be. Thank y'all for blessing my life. I love ALL of you.

To the rest of the family and friends:

I want to thank both sides of my family and friends for being there to help guide me along my journey and through this thing we call life. Each of you have played a part in my life, rather if I mentioned it or not. I thank you just for being you and loving me. I love y'all!

Table of Contents

FORWARD: BY DAPHAROAH69
PAGE A-1

PROLOGUE:
PAGE 9

PART 1: THE CALM BEFORE THE STORM
PAGE 13

CHAPTER 1: INTRODUCTION
PAGE 15

CHAPTER 2: WHERE IT ALL BEGAN
PAGE 25

PART 2: ENTERING THE STORM
PAGE 29

CHAPTER 3: THE CALL THAT CHANGED IT ALL
PAGE 31

CHAPTER 4: MY NEW ALTERED LIFE
PAGE 37

CHAPTER 5: READY OR NOT HERE WE GO
PAGE 49

CHAPTER 6: FIRST DAY IN HELL'S PLAYGROUND
PAGE 63

CHAPTER 7: THE DEVIL THOUGHT HE HAD ME
PAGE 81

CHAPTER 8: A WEEK OF STRESS THERAPY
PAGE 95

CHAPTER 9: FINALLY, I BELIEVE
PAGE 101

PART 3: THROUGH THE STORM COMES OPEN DOORS
PAGE 109

CHAPTER 10: THIS IS THE DAY THE LORD HAS MADE
PAGE 111

CHAPTER 11: MY SECOND CHANCE AT LIFE
PAGE 129

CHAPTER 12: ONE STEP FORWARD TWO STEPS BACK
PAGE 135

CHAPTER 13: BEING A BLESSING
PAGE 143

CHAPTER 14: BECOMING A LIVING TESTIMONY
PAGE 151

EPILOGUE:
PAGE 159

ACKNOWLEDGEMENTS:
PAGE 165

COLLAGE OF PHOTOS:
PAGE 169-171

Forward

By Dapharoah69

A

> TO WHOM MUCH IS GIVEN, MUCH WILL BE REQUIRED...
> (LUKE 12:48)

With warm regards, Welcome to "Becoming A Living Testimony." I truly hope that these humble words find you, the reader, in the best of health, family and good spirits. I'm your host, award-winning, bestselling author Dapharoah69. I'm not gonna bore you with my professional resume, for this very moment, this event, isn't about me. With joy and urgency, I want to share a few words with you, the reader, that will set the tone for the journey you're about to embark on…a journey into an incredible mind…a visionary beyond anything you could ever imagine.

That Visionary was my brother from another mother.

At this exact moment, I literally just finished performing with multi-platinum artist Gavin Degraw at the 2019 Orange Bowl Half-Time Show. Hard Rock Stadium. I was one of about seventy dancers on the field, making our Prime-Time debut. I'm drained from intense rehearsals over the last few days, but I put that same drive and passion into this outstanding work of art.

I have a question for you. Are you Living or Existing? Have you ever existed in this thing called Life, but haven't truly lived? You accomplish set goals, but still felt like you could do more. Well, I was one of those people that used to exist, but never fully lived. I used to put others before my own well-being. Writing was the interruption of everything.

For me, writing is a catharsis…a painful journey wrought with peril, sadness and tears. Writing, for me, for ARTavius, is a form of ventilation and therapy. A way out, a way to cope and deal with the pressures of our individual lives…

I think of the many delightful phone conversations between me and "Tay." And we've shared many. Felt like I knew him my entire life. He's a fresh breath of air after suffocation. An energetic ball of energy that rubs off on you

B

until it *becomes* you. That's Tay! He's a great listener and highly intelligent. He knows his purpose and what he wants out of life. After you finish reading his testimony, penned by his mastery, told in his words, from his candid experiences, you, too, will walk away with bouts of empowerment and a better understanding of a kindred soul that suffered from kidney disease since he was very young. His strength and resilience will astound you…

If I am going to accept the absolute honor of penning the *Forward* to ARTavius Veasey's invigorating life story, a realistic glimpse, I will have to start from the beginning.

About eight, maybe nine years ago I met ARTavius, "Tay," through Miko, owner of Meak Productions; a LGBTQ talent agency based in Atlanta. I was the Agency's *first* literary talent of the year in 2010. Tay was the talented graphic designer behind some of Miko's campaigns shortly after. I was anxious to meet Tay because of how highly Miko spoke of him. When we finally connected, we hit it off instantly.

He reminded me of someone, but I couldn't put my finger on it. It wasn't until me and my husband John's impromptu three-day trip to Atlanta, where I was receiving a literary award for my achievements back in 2015 as a member of the Elite 300 Brotherhood, that I figured out exactly who Tay reminded me of…

The fact that a mutual friend, Kurt, set us up with a luxurious stay at the world-famous Ritz Carlton was awesome in itself. Suspiciously, Kurt kept teasing us about a "surprise." He also said that someone was driving to us from another state, just to meet us, adding to this "surprise."

Mind you. I hate surprises…

C

A few hours later, there was a knock on our hotel room door. I didn't remember who answered it, but the sight of ARTavius, in the flesh, caused me to explode with joy. It was one of the best days of my life. Like attracted like. He gave the best hug. I could still feel his arms around me all these years later. He was a huge fan of my work. I was an even bigger fan of his artistic genius. Over the next few days, we bonded. "Tay" became my brother in every sense of the word.

I remember his request. He said that when he wrote his first book, his testimony, he wanted me to help him with it. I most surely accepted.

A few years later, late 2019, out of the blue, I received an unexpected call from Tay. It was a few weeks before Orange Bowl Half-Time Show rehearsals. He was excited, telling me that his memoir was completed. I kept my word and dived right into editing that night. When I read about his struggle (I read it four times before I edited a single word) confirmed who he reminded me of.

My little brother, Lonnie Wilson. Pictured above in the striped shirt with me, my husband and my baby brother, NCO Kelvin Brown, Airforce.

Both Tay and Lonnie suffered kidney disease and were treated through dialysis since they were very young. My brother was about 17 years old when both of his kidneys mysteriously shut down, destroying my family.

The pain, the frustration, the helplessness, the exhaustion was undeniably unbearable. I remember volunteering to donate one of my kidneys, but I wasn't compatible.

I thought about the times I took my brother to dialysis three days a week and picked him up once his treatment was over, sometimes having his daughters, my nieces, in tow with me.

The ordeal weighed down on our mother, but since she was a praying woman, God always showed us favor and provided him the support system he needed. I remember when he received his kidney transplant.

I remember when, years later, he lost the kidney and had to be put back on the waiting list. I also remember how good God was. My brother received another transplant shortly before his birthday a couple years later.

I remember me and my brother weren't very close. We hardly spoke and rarely called each other.

I remember when Lonnie moved to Michigan to start a new life. I remember, shortly after, he wound up with a ventilator down his throat because of a tooth infection and he flatlined.

With tears in my eyes, I remember me and my other brother, named Taye as well, drove twenty-three hours with me from Miami, Florida to Pontiac, Michigan to be by our brother's side. I remember a nurse refused to let Lonnie die. My mother was destroyed, so I had to be strong for my entire immediate family and it was nearly impossible to do. This was my little brother. He's already endured so much. He was only in his late twenties.

Abruptly, his nurse jumped on top of him and beat him in the chest till he came back to us. He flatlined again. Twice. My brother Taye and I broke to pieces, a complete breakdown in front of all the doctors and staff. My brother died again, yet that same nurse jumped back on top of him with that same energy. And she pounded him back to life again.

Now he lives a full life, in spite of his recent leg amputation.

After all the prayers, blood, sweat, tears, and energy I put into my literary craft over the past 34 years, I have reached an epiphany. One I couldn't ignore. My body of work means nothing if I can't be of service to someone other than my immediate family, my husband or even myself. To be of service to someone outside of my "circle."

Presently, I face that tabernacle of purpose. I say *tabernacle* because my Heavenly Father has engulfed my dwelling place with aplomb and meaning. I was being tested.

A test of selfless abandon, in Jesus name, whom I refer to as Yashua, after granting me so much…

What was the test and the task?

Will I help a fellow brother with his purpose?

Will I assist Tay Veasey with getting to the level of visibility that no one helped me with?

Will I do any and everything in my power to help him with his vision, after all the opportunistic doors slammed in my face during the Genesis of my rise up the literary ladder so long ago?

Will I treat his book as if I was writing, prepping and releasing my very own, staying up all night, burning the midnight oil, calling him with questions, better understanding his agenda, until he achieved perfection?

You see, I have a problem with rejection. I have a problem with the word "no" when it comes to my voice being heard. So, when publishers rejected me, I found my own way. And that "way" has become an open door for "Becoming A Living Legend" the way James Baldwin, E. Lynn Harris, Langston Hughes and countless other black literary legends did for next the generation of independent writers like me.

An Invisible Life was a self-published book E Lynn Harris sold out of his car before he inked a major publishing deal.

That "way" gave me the experience to treat ARTavius' voice with class, decency and respect so he avoids the very doors that once slammed in my face. His voice is protected and preserved because of my own brother's struggle with kidney disease, so I can relate whole-heartedly…

I told myself that I would do what I had to do to publish my own stories and teach Tay that as well. To not rely on anyone to fend or fight for my art, my craft. If it was meant to be it would be.

To incite change you must illicit change from within. I did it through prayer and faith in my ability.

Now was the time to…pay it forward.

To the incomparable, magnetically talented ARTavius Veasey.

To say that I'm deeply moved to be a part of a spellbinding, inspirational body of non-fiction literature is an understatement. I can remember how I felt when bestselling author Lee Hayes wrote the Forward to my autobiography "The Kingdom." I feel that same excitement for ARTavius.

In Tay's words comes a story of loss and perseverance. He refused to accept the perils threatening his life and his emotional state.

Eloquently presented with love, vindication and grandeur. "Becoming A Living Testimony" is a national treasure I had the pleasure of reading and editing before it was released to the world. I was extremely careful not to change or alter his voice.

ARTavius project came at a time, last year, I was at the lowest point of my life…

I had God and prayer. That mustard seed has become my life force and my beacon of light.

Before the accolades, the notoriety, the book sales, the con artists…my publishing journey started with just one word from my blinking cursor on a laptop my best friend David bought me when I was homeless.

Only I didn't tell a soul that I was. Resting on a sleeping bag in the middle of an old Airforce housing section that has long become woods, towering trees and forgotten streets. Presently, it has been replenished and turned into the Homestead Air Reserved Park.

But seventeen years ago, it was the place I wrote my first book…None of that mattered last year. When I told God that I was giving Him back the gift of writing. That I didn't want it anymore because of what I lost. I suffered the greatest depression of my life…

Then I got an unexpected call from ARTavius Veasey.

Somebody forgot to tell me that when God sets something in motion, even you can't stop it. When you set a goal, and put in the work, God aligns the very people in your path to make sure that it happens. We don't know who they are until we encounter them via some form of confirmation.

It's gonna take a miracle to capture ARTavius, a beautiful, mesmerizing, gifted juggernaut, in all of his essence.

Survivor. Inspiration. Breathtaking Actor. Creative Director. Graphic Artist. Gold Medalist. To say anything beyond those words would reveal all of his incomparable hats and slashes. If Lauryn is a rapper slash actor, then add about ten more slashes to Mr. Veasey.

There wasn't a warehouse, a studio or a stadium big enough to house all of his talent and gifts. He's a multi-faceted media empire, confined in a tiny body.

On the surface, he's a humble, determined soul. But before I was to know all of this, before I was to know of his struggle, before I was to know about his stage plays, his philanthropy or his penmanship, I simply knew him as ARTavius Veasey. The graphic artist. The brother from another mother. The inspiration.

Upon meeting him, I knew that I wouldn't be the same. As it turns out, God doesn't make any mistakes.

ARTavius is a zenith, a somewhat otherworldly occurrence. Yet his entire journey, the way both of our individual lives and struggles meshed into the birth of this very Forward, was a testament that something we have endured or survived could be the catharsis for another person's healing.

As "Becoming A Living Testimony" has done for my very own personal development, it is my wish that his testimony inspires you to be, become and transcend into your greatest self.

Through Tay's vision, I learned to love my brother Lonnie all over again.

And for that, thank you…

I am my Brother's Keeper.

With love, honor and respect,

IF YOU REFUSE TO BE A BLESSING, (BE OF SERVICE)
AFTER REAPING ITS BENEFIT, (DONE IN VAIN)
YOUR PETALS WILL BECOME LIKE ASH; THEY WITHER AND BLACKEN...FORGOTTEN
(DAPHAROAH69)

MY HUSBAND, JOHN WILSON. ARTAVIUS. ME.

PROLOGUE:

10 BECOMING A LIVING TESTIMONY

Before I present my emotional and life changing testimony via the following pages, I would like to first give glory and thanks to my Heavenly Father, Jesus Christ. Thank you for giving me the opportunity and the platform to share my testimony with the world. Without Him, none of this would be possible.

As I promised Him when I was on dialysis...

> *"Lord…if you help me through this…*
> *I PROMISE I will share my story*
> *and do everything in my power to encourage*
> *those on their journey*
> *towards transplantation."*

Through God's grace and favor, it has been 10+ years, post-transplant. Purposely, I waited after my ten-year anniversary to release my story. I pray that my testimony becomes a **BLESSING** to those living with kidney disease. Whether if you know of someone, family or friend, that has kidney disease or if you are diagnosed with the disease, I hope you, the reader, experience my life through the pages of my personal journal.

Living with kidney disease wasn't a crystal stair, but I have become stronger, despite opposition…

It is my intent that you become inspired, empowered, and ultimately, motivated. There's **HOPE** and *every* issue has a **RESOLVE**…

AND IT'S WITHIN YOU!

I assure you that it is.

It is not my intent to scare you with my testimony, make you feel any pity for me or my situation…nor do I mean to make you cry. My story is meant to heal those who may be broken.

Wholeheartedly, I thank *you* (the reader) for purchasing this book and taking the time to read about my journey.

May the Lord continue to bless you and I wish nothing but love and positivity over your life.

Without further ado, let's begin shall we! I would like to start this journey by introducing myself and giving you a quick glimpse into my early childhood…

PART 1:

THE CALM BEFORE THE STORM

14 BECOMING A LIVING TESTIMONY

CHAPTER 1:

INTRODUCTION

16 BECOMING A LIVING TESTIMONY

Hey, y'all! My name was ARTavius Veasey. I was born in Memphis, Tennessee on February 21, 1990. I was raised there as well. Thinking back over my early years, I fondly remembered how often I was around my loving family and friends. There was always some type of party or get together; plenty of fun and laughter that lasted until we all met up again on the next holiday or family get together. There was never a dull or boring moment. Even though both of my parents weren't in the same household, they did their part in providing for me.

However, having young parents created an unwarranted and unforeseen segue. Their absence opened the door for my beautiful grandmother, Shirley Veasey, whom I refer to as "Gma" (pronounced "Jee-Ma"), to not only raise me, but fill the void left by my parents.

Not taking anything away from my parents, because I believe they did the best they knew how in raising a child at such a young age, and I loved them both, but my Gma helped set the tone for my upbringing.

When I thought about my childhood, I fondly remembered being around my Gma Shirley for the most part. I was always accompanied and spoiled by her and Aunt Wanda. If my grandmother wasn't around or at home, Aunt Wanda was always there.

Honestly, still to this day, at twenty-eight years old, they still spoil me. I couldn't be more thankful for those two women. They'd taught me a great deal about life and set the foundation for everything I know today.

As a child, it was awesome having a grandmother that was an upbeat socialite. I got the chance to see and witness a lot of things.

Grandma was outgoing, loved to have fun and regularly entertained her friends. I believed that was where my comical humor came from, besides my hilarious father.

One thing I'd learned and admired about Gma Shirley was the love she had for her girls, Ms. Bertha and Ms. Georgia Brown. Loyalty. They had a real sisterhood. Those three seemed to be inseparable and they loved hanging out at their favorite spot, Parkway Grill.

They always had fun and enjoyed each other's company. I loved listening to their funny stories. Their taste in music was impeccable. Ultimately, I picked up on some of their habits and wisdom.

The wisdom they occasionally instilled in me didn't make sense at the time, but I never forgot it. Suffice it to say, I knew it could be useful later in life.

Both of Gma Shirley's friends treated me so nice. Just being included in their conversations made me feel like I was a special part of their friend circle.

Like any other spoiled child (i.e. by a loved one or was a daddy's girl or momma's boy) knows, you always wanted to be around that special person. **NO MATTER WHAT!**

Separation was always an issue for me and caused an ugly tantrum on my behalf. It was uncontrollable and very uncomfortable. For me, during my early childhood, I was grand momma's baby; she was my other mother when my biological mother wasn't around.

You can ask anyone in my family today. I was crazy about my grandmother. I couldn't stand being away from her. I was so in love and obsessed with her. Her wisdom was unbelievable.

Every day with her was a different story and a different lesson learned and lovingly acquired. She taught me about morals, decency and respect. And more wisdom. I was always learning something new and soaking it all in like a sponge.

As I grew a little older and got into daycare and pre-k, it caused me to be away from my grandmother during the weekdays, but I was back at her house on the weekends.

When she dropped me off at daycare on those dreadful Monday mornings that came like clockwork, I knew I wouldn't see her for a long time (in my mind) because she had to go to work and I would have a fit.

Nobody could stop me from crying, but her. It got to the point where I didn't want to go to school. I'd rather go to work with her.

She said I really didn't like being away from her. She had a memorable story she used to always tell me about how she kept me from crying when dropping me off at daycare.

"The only way I could keep you from crying, when I dropped you off, was showing you how to count down the days, we'll see each other again, using your fingers."

She held up my hands with her own.

Gma: "You went to school this many and got this many to go. I'll say...you went to school with these three (pointing at three of my fingers) and you got two more to go (pushing fingers down to show two left).

"When you get down to that last finger...you know that that is your last day of school and my last day of work for the week. That's when you first learned how to subtract."

There was always something new to learn or grasp when it came to my grandmother. She was always big on education and "getting your lesson done, *first,* before you play" as she would say.

Outside of daycare and early grade school, she was my tutor, study buddy, guidance counselor, mentor and my mother…all at the same time.

I'd learned so much from her. Nonetheless, she was still all those people in one, till this day.

I couldn't be more grateful and blessed to have a woman like my grandmother who was a single mother and raised three kids on her own.

Even though she was going through her own personal problems, she never let it come between her children (including myself).

Fiercely, she made sure we all had what we needed, plus some. She was such a powerful and strong-willed black woman.

It amazed me how she did it all.

Now at seventy-four years young, she's still healthy and gets around like she did in the good ole days. She always and still was that person I looked up to and wanted to be as I continuously grew and matured.

The way she shared some of her resources with her fellow man and gave to people in need remained unmatched...

No matter what was going on in your life or what you needed, if Shirley had it or if she could share some advice, she would do so...without a doubt.

I strived to be just like her, yet I desired to forge my own path and blazed my own trail...respectively setting an example for the next generation to follow.

I learned to treat people the way I wanted to be treated; I loved thy neighbor as if they were family and I was a blessing to others in whichever way I could.

Growing up mostly around my grandmother, I had a plethora of stories and lessons in life that she'd taught me over the years...

However, some of the most important lessons in life that I'd learned from her was about the importance of family and in her love my confidence began to blossom like a rose in the Memphis sunshine.

Family...she was BIG on family; she was such a family person; she would give her last to help family out. She used to always tell me how family was so important.

"No matter how far we may go or grow apart, or how successful we may become, you can always come home and depend on family to be there. Always stay focused to achieve your dreams and know where you are going, but never forget where you came from; because at the end of the day when we ain't got nobody...we always have family. We're all we got!"

Good or bad. No family was perfect.

Confidence...We've had multiple talks and discussions about confidence due to me struggling with my own...as I got older, but Gma Shirley never failed to encourage and uplift me when I was down.

She told me, "Confidence must be instilled early in life. I tried to be sure to instill confidence within all my children, because if they could believe and put forth the effort, then they could do and be whatever they wanted to be.

"It doesn't matter what you want to be. You be the best at it. I don't care if you want to be a garbage man...You better be the best one they got!

"No matter what walk of life you're going into, your good is not better until your better is best.

"'Good, Better, Best; never let it rest, till your good gets better, and your better is best'."

-JJ McGowan.
Gma Shirley's Principal
at Hernando Central High School.

In your journey through life, things will change; and so many people do just enough to achieve one goal and enough to get by.

But if you put that little effort to go even further, things would be much different for your life, but you got to put forth the effort.

You can't just do what somebody says and be content with that, put forth the extra effort...

"Like I was saying about garbage men; they are only required to pick up this tub of garbage, that tub of garbage and so on.

"But if you go as far as picking up the garbage that's on the side of the tubs that's been neglected or garbage off the street and throwing it in with the other trash, then that's putting forth the extra effort.

"Cleaning up a little bit better. The extra effort stands out! When you're doing more than required that'll help you stand out amongst the rest."

And there you have it, folks!

I wanted to give you a highlight of who I am and my early childhood. Hopefully you all have a good enough picture on what my life was like at an early age, before my affliction…

The calm before the storm…

So, turn the page and continue reading my story. Have an open mind as you travel with me into the storm

that completely changed my life and made me the person I am today.
 A Victor...!

CHAPTER 2:

WHERE IT ALL BEGAN

"**AND HERE HE IS!**" The doctor said joyfully, as she raised my timid body to show to my young parents. It was the 21st of February. The time: 9:26 a.m. The place: The Med hospital in Memphis, Tennessee.

Prematurely delivered at thirty-four weeks, weighing three pounds, eleven ounces, I came earlier than expected. I could fit perfectly in the cuff of my dad's hand.

Being born to a mother who struggled with kidney disease, there was an inevitable chance that I, too, may develop it later in life. I was held in ICU (intensive care unit) for a few months until the doctors felt I was healthy enough to finally go home.

Once the doctor cleared my parents to take me home, life went on...

After a couple of months passed, things were going just fine. I did the normal things premature infants did. The extra doctor visits, checkups, routine shots and close care from family was due to me having a low immune system.

As time went by, things seemed to be going well.

By the age of three, I was active as ever; walking, talking and getting into all types of stuff was the norm.

Then came the time for my six-month routine checkup. Momma was at ease due to me being healthy and not sick as much, so I was making progress.

However, just evaluating me from the outside... everything looked fine, but once the doctor came in with my chart and results from my recent test, everything wasn't okay.

In fact, it was devastating...

The doctor patiently disclosed that my body was developing kidney disease. I was diagnosed with the sickle cell trait as well, confirming that the trait and kidney disease was hereditary from her.

Confirming my parents' worst, inevitable fear...

"So how long will it be before he has to go on dialysis?" my momma asked, sadly.

"Well, I can't say an exact date right now," the attentive doctor responded. "The best we could do is just continue to monitor the disease as it develops and make decisions as we go. We're not going to jump to conclusions yet.

"Just pay attention to his behavior and monitor his urine," the doctor continued. "Occasionally ask if it burns or hurts...If so, bring him back here and we can run tests and make further decisions from there. But right now, other than that, he's as healthy as he could be."

So even though the doctor was trying to keep my mother from jumping to conclusions, she couldn't help it. She'd been through the process already, years before I was born, so she knew what to expect when it came to the kidneys.

As time went by, everything was good.

I was happy being a kid and experiencing life.

The disease was developing, but at a slow pace.

The doctors didn't have to do much outside of my quarterly checkups...

Inevitably, that was about to change...

PART 2:

ENTERING THE STORM

30 BECOMING A LIVING TESTIMONY

CHAPTER 3:

The Call that Changed It All

32 BECOMING A LIVING TESTIMONY

The year was 2004; a year I'd never forget. I was thirteen years old, about to finish my last year of middle school. Soon, I'd be a high schooler. I was excited and so ready to finally be able to say I was in high school. I heard people say high school was where you transitioned from a teenager to a young adult.

I was excited for this "transition", or so I thought.

Healthwise, everything was okay for the most part. I was sick here and there, but nothing alarming. Just the common cold. I was doing pretty good.

Nothing too crazy, right?

Well, let's just say that all went left field when I received "The Call" that changed it all.

It was a normal, uneventful evening. Momma and my other grandmama (not my Gma Shirley) picked me up from Southwind Middle School.

We stayed right around the corner from my school, so it wasn't a long drive back to the house.

We were laughing and joking around (as we always did) until we pulled into the driveway.

Abruptly, my mother's phone rang. Based on her expression, I knew it was somebody important.

Willing herself, she turned down the radio and beautifully transitioned into (what I called) "the operator voice."

The *operator voice* was a tone you used when you were disinterested in said phone call, saying sarcastic things like, "…Uh-huh, okay, yes sir/ma'am, yes okay, un-huh…," etcetera…

When she hung up the phone, her eyes welled with huge tears. It rocked me deep within. She looked at me. I was sitting in the middle of the backseat, wrought with confusion.

"What? What's wrong?" I asked, exasperated.

No comment.

She just stared at me, quietly...

The dead silence was deafening.

"Who was that? What happened?" I continued to ask.

"That was your doctor" she responded.

"Okay...what did he say?" I was nervous, my heart pounding out of my chest. "Is something wrong?"

"Your kidneys are getting worse...you will have to start taking medicine and possibly go on dialysis," she reluctantly answered, crying even harder.

Once I heard those life changing words, that I had to take medication and possibly undergo dialysis, it felt like my world stopped.

Just like that.

Boom!

In an instant.

The unnerving numb feeling that washed over me like a tsunami taunted me. It was the worst news of my life.

All I could think about was how my life was about to change. From that point on.

A gazillion thoughts buzzed around my cranium.

How would my friends react?

Would I be able to go back to school?

How would this affect my body. And many other things.

I honestly didn't know what to think. I was extremely terrified.

She continued to cry out loud.

The time we spent in the car was uncomfortable. For us both.

As we sat in the drive-way, Momma hadn't uttered a word. Was she feeling powerless in an uncontrollable situation?

What would my dad think once Momma informed him of the catastrophic news?

Suffice it to say, when we entered the house, the silence was deafening to my ears once again, giving me brief flash backs of her demeanor and my unease after "The Call.".

Momma barely glanced at me, yet I was watching her like a hawk, confined to my own private thoughts.

She never even asked me how I felt about my illness.

Retreating to my room, my sacred place, I was like a log on still waters. Motionless as I sat on my bed.

I thought deeply about the changes I was about to endure. Would I be strong enough to persevere or would I give up on myself?

I was much too strong to throw in the towel.

I had no choice but to face my fears.

I really didn't fully understand the depth of it all. At that checkpoint in my life I'd never felt so down and so disappointed...

All I knew was...whatever happened...I got to deal with it...

Because there's no turning back now.

CHAPTER 4:

MY NEW ALTERED LIFE

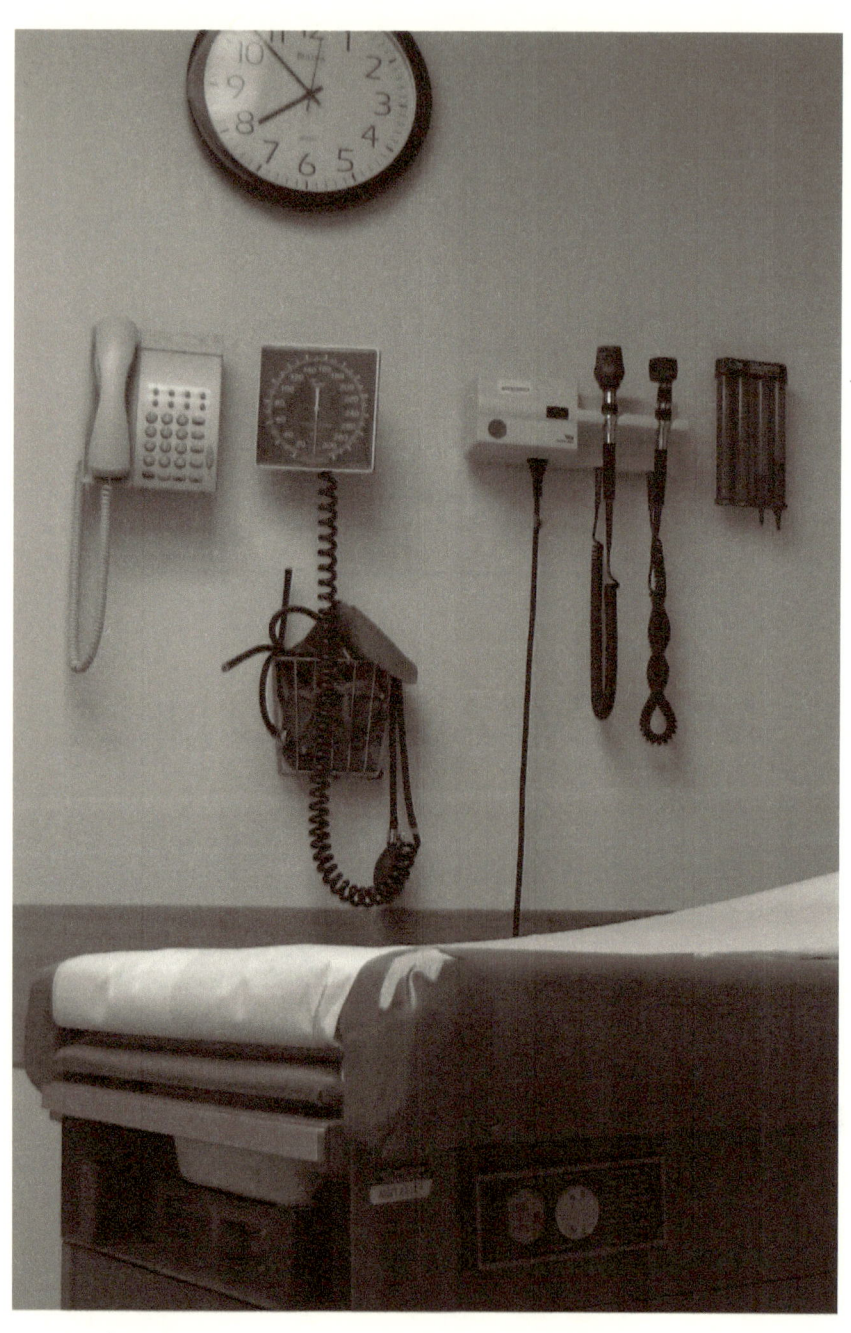

38 BECOMING A LIVING TESTIMONY

That heartbreaking, dreadful day inevitably came like a thief in the night. January 6, 2004; the first day of the rest of my altered life. This is the day that I met with my physician, Dr. Ault. She was going to counsel, educate and guide me through this life altering process; a process that will challenge every part of my being...

Unlike anything I could ever imagine...

Starting dialysis...

To add insult to injury, as if losing my kidneys wasn't a devastating blow to my gut, I would have to take all types of medication for the rest of my days....

Who knew the effects those pills would have on my body in the long run? I was sure there have been a few people with kidney disease that weren't strong enough to face a life dependent on dialysis machines, but what choice do I have?

A wise man once said that pain was love.

Well...I was about to find out.

I was too motivated to give up. I knew in my heart that I would continue moving forward and not let this invigorating experience stop me from wanting to endure and persevere...

I did love me. A great responsibility came with that. I must protect my mental state of mind because a situation such as this one was enough to challenge your faith and your sanity...

With a God that performed miracles and a Gma named Shirley, I was going to be just fine...

Nonetheless, I refused to die before my life truly started, so I would face this head on. The key to adversity was to work harder...

I had kidney disease; kidney disease didn't have me.

It helped, also, that my mother went through the same process before I was even a fetus, so I was already prepared for this day for a very long time.

But now that the day reared its ugly head, any weapon formed against me...

Shall not prosper!

Dr. Bettinna Ault was a pediatric nephrologist. She specialized in kidney disease affecting children. I look her over as we greeted each other. She was a Caucasian woman with short blonde hair. Her smile was infectious.

"Hey, Artavius...! How are *you* doing?" Dr. Ault asked me.

"I'm alright...*try'na* stay positive" I responded. I was a little uneasy.

"Well, that's good! You're off to a great start. We're going to take good care of you..."

"Okay..."

"You're scheduled for your first treatment next Monday, the 13th," she went on. "...but you're scheduled for surgery this coming Saturday morning. Your lines are going to be implanted."

"What do you mean by *my lines*"? I asked, a bit disoriented about it all. It was a lot to process.

"The surgical term is 'dialysis catheter'," she went on, "but a lot of patients call it 'lines'. Anyways, it's a catheter or a tube used to transport your blood to and from the dialysis machine, filtering you. Your dialysis catheter consists of two tubes...known as 'lumens'. One is called the 'venous' and the other is called 'arterial...'"

As she described the process of my upcoming surgery, it freaked me out a little bit.

After a few moments I became surprisingly calm.

I didn't think too much into it.

Prior to my doctor's appointment, I had a heartfelt talk with God. I'd said to him, "If it's your will…I accept what I need to survive. Lord, I trust you and I know there's a reason for it all.

"Amen."

Yes, I would be honest and say that I was terrified, but my grandmother always taught me that everything happened for a reason. We may not understand it in the beginning, but before your storm was over…

You would understand why.

Dr. Ault broke my chain of thought.

"Okay, so after your surgery…we'll bring you back to your room to do a few tests," said Dr. Ault, bringing me back to the present moment, "…and check to make sure the lines don't blow or get clogged."

"Blow? Like blow up?" I asked nervously, thinking of an explosion.

"No, no…, like a tire blowing out. It's useless, "she explained.

"Oh, okay."

Phew! I was like, Hold on now…! This thing can blow up. Inside my body? No ma'am! I thought to myself.

I looked at her sternly. "You sure this is safe?"

She chuckled. "Yes, it's safe. And I understand your concern. I'm glad you are asking questions, though. That means you're paying attention."

"Okay…but what happens after the lines have a blowout?" I asked out of curiosity. "How do y'all fix them?"

"In order to fix them, we will have to surgically remove them and put in new ones."

I sighed. "Goodness. I hope that don't happen to me…going through this twice. No, ma'am!"

"I hope not either, Artavius. We're going to perform the procedure properly in hopes that it doesn't blow."

"Okay."

"Your assigned nurse will come in every couple of hours, or as needed, to flush out your lines. Keeping them clean and clear."

My brows rose. "What do you mean by 'flushing...'"

"We're going to connect a syringe to your lines and push saline intravenously through your tubes. Saline is a solution of salt in water...That's it. Sunday, your surgical doctors and I will come visit you. To see how you are feeling. We'll make sure that everything is good and ready for your first treatment Monday morning.

"But as far as dialysis goes, you'll have treatment for three hours, three days a week. The days are mainly Monday, Wednesday and Friday. If anything changes, we'll let you know. At first glance, the dialysis process may scare you, but we have very helpful nurses there to assist you if you have any discomfort or questions.

"They will also walk you through the process more in depth when they hook you up to the machine," she says. "Your lines will be implanted in your chest. That form of dialysis is called 'hemodialysis.'"

"Oh, okay. I know my momma had her lines placed in her arm, and the way her arm looked was scary."

"Yes, your mom mentioned that. She didn't want your lines implanted in your arm. She chose your chest instead," she confirmed.

"Thank you for that because the arm thing looks scary. Are there other places you can have your lines besides the arm and chest?" I asked.

I didn't mean to turn this into an interview, but I just had to know.

"Yes. Sometimes you may see a kidney patient on hemodialysis and the lines are in his or her neck. Another location for lines is the stomach. That form is called peritoneal dialysis."

"Oh, okay. I didn't know they all had different names. I thought it was all one," I replied.

"No, there are only two main types of dialysis, but they each have a few locations the lines could be placed. With that being said, the next thing I want to talk to you about is your medication. It is very important that you stay on top of taking your meds every day, on time…"

"Yes, I know. My mom told me how important my meds are already," I interrupted.

"Okay, great…once your transplant takes place and you have the new kidney, your T4 cells are going to try and fight it off because the implanted kidney is something that wasn't there before; it's a foreign object. Your immune system will treat it as an infection and try to kill it. The meds serve as defense mechanisms. They shield the new kidney against your body trying to reject it. They also keep you healthy."

"I understand," I said.

"You take your meds daily, the better your kidney health will be. If you fall behind on your meds or stop taking them, it could cause your body to reject the kidney. You will have to go back on dialysis and wait until another kidney is available for transplantation. I'm sure your mother told you how hard and long you may have to wait if placed on the waiting list again."

"Yea…she said it feels like forever."

"Well, each patient is different. As of now, there are over eighty thousand people waiting on an organ transplant. Every month…over one thousand people are added to the national waiting list. But there are cases concerning living donors that received a kidney quicker than others that's been on the list for years."

"Oh, wow. I didn't know all of that." I was in momentary shock.

"Yeah. It's very important that you take care of the new kidney. It'll be hard putting you back on the waiting list if you lose the kidney via not taking your meds. Your chances are slim for a second kidney. There are thousands of people still looking to receive their first one.

"Just keep that in mind," she continued. "Also, if the patient has a family member or friend who are a match and their bodies are healthy enough to bare the surgery, we could bypass the waiting list all together and get the new kidney directly versus getting it from a John Doe."

"Yeah, my momma got her kidney from this guy in Portland, Oregon," I said.

"Exactly. The donor could be here in the United States or from another country," she implied.

"Right. Now what I'm having a problem understanding is this, is the new kidney coming from a deceased person?" I wanted to know.

"In some cases, yes. A kidney may come from a deceased person, but like I said earlier, there are living donors as well."

"Wait, so you can live with just one kidney?" I asked. She had my full attention.

"Absolutely. A lot of people don't know that because of the myth and stigma. As long as *you're* healthy you can live with just one kidney and be completely fine. Doing the same fun things, you did when you had two."

"Oh, my God! I didn't know that!" I was actually intrigued.

"Yeah, a lot of people don't know. That's why you see a lot of representatives advocating to educate the masses about kidney disease. Encouraging them to become future organ donors. To be sure that its marked on their driver's licenses through the Department of Motor Vehicles. In the unfortunate event that something was to fatally happen, their vital organs can help save lives."

"Wow, I never knew that either," I affirmed.

"Yeah. You'll be surprised how many people don't know that. We're not trying to make everyone give away their organs. We just want people to know that when we've passed on, our organs can still be used to help those in need. We don't need our organs once we're gone.

Ultimately, it's up to the individual if he or she wants to become an organ donor," she further explained.

"Right. I completely understand." I agreed.

"If you could spread the word and help us educate people about transplantation and becoming potential organ donors," she gleefully suggested. "We all would appreciate it."

"Of course. Anything I can do to help. I'm a part of the family now." I smiled.

"Thank you."

She continued. "This is how I look at it. If you want your kidney to last as long as possible, you must take your meds to protect it. Once you get into the groove of taking them, it'll be like clockwork. In regard to being on dialysis, you have to be on a precise diet for the duration of your treatments."

Respectively, Dr. Ault begun to tell me a lot when it came to my fluids and diet. She suggested that I kept track of the amount of liquids I drank and what I ate.

More specifically, I had to limit my intake of certain foods and avoid foods and drinks that was high in potassium, phosphorus and sodium.

For example: oranges, orange juice, potatoes, tomatoes, salt, salty foods, chips, whole wheat bread, pasta, dairy products, fish, certain meats, and dark colored drinks (including sweet tea, vegetable juices and sports drinks).

She continued to tell me the reason why I had to track my liquid intake. It was because excess fluid buildup in the body may cause swelling and weight gain.

Changes in blood pressure could be potentially hazardous.

She wanted me to watch my blood pressure levels. High blood pressure already ran in my family.

She went over other things regarding my diet. She encouraged me to talk with my renal dietitian for more tips and for ways to help my journey remain smooth and steady.

Now as I was listening to her and following along on my paperwork, it felt as if she was putting me on temporary punishment.

I was thinking to myself, heavily, that these folks were trying to kill me, for real.

I was barely eighty pounds...and they wanted me to go on a diet?

Were they trying to make me so thin that a gust of wind could blow me away?

I was nowhere near overweight.

If you asked me…I was closer to being underweight and anorexic more than anything. I knew that it would be a struggle to give up or limit some of my favorite things to eat and drink. What I once enjoyed was now compromising.

It was a lot to take in, right after being introduced to those two pills I was bound to take till the day I died.

I was going to need God and the whole Salvation Army to help me through this one.

"And lastly, before we wrap it up," she went on, "I want to talk to you, briefly, about home school. I'm not saying that all patients do home schooling, but some do. With the treatments being three days a week, you're going to feel tired and drained for the most part.

"Other side effects may include muscle cramps and itchy skin. It may be hard to stay asleep once you go to bed at night. You may experience insomnia. There could be bone or joint pain, dry mouth and anxiety. The aforementioned things may cause you to suffer in class. You might get behind on your work.

"But don't get discouraged…" She encouraged me with a huge smile. "We're not trying to scare you or take you away from your friends. You have options. You now know what they are. I'm giving you a heads up about what may happen while receiving treatment. If you get your kidney early, while still in high school, you could possibly go back and graduate with your class and friends, so don't beat yourself up about being home schooled, okay?"

"Okay" I answered. Overwhelmed with emotion. It seemed like a blur. Like I was in another realm of consciousness.

I sat before Dr. Ault, indifferent.

All her information would never leave me.

"Before we finish..." She broke the silence. "...do you have any questions?"

"No, I'm good..." Of course, it was an absolute lie. I found it nerve wracking. The bile in my throat matched the tingling in my limbs. Information overload.

"Great. Wait here. I'm going to check to make sure that you're ready to go and everything is set before we let you leave today. I'll be right back," she said, walking out of the room.

As the door closed behind Dr. Ault, I felt like I was on the verge of a nervous breakdown. It seemed like everything was falling apart.

At this point I was completely terrified for the next chapter in my life.

Everything was changing...in the blink of an eye.

Thinking about how my friends and favorite teachers would take it if I had to be home schooled.

Would my friends still hang out with me?

Support or help me?

Would my teachers give me more work?

A million things zoomed through my head.

Yes, I felt some type of way about the whole dialysis thing. Felt like I was forced into it.

There was one thing that I knew, though...

The Lord didn't put on me more than I could bare.

There was no turning back now.

CHAPTER 5:

READY OR NOT HERE WE GO!

Before I could exhale, Saturday, January 11, 2004 ran up on me without preamble. The day I was admitted into hell. Mom and I were sitting in the waiting area, waiting for somebody from the medical staff to come take us to my room on the sixth floor.

Nonetheless, today was quite rough. I wasn't too happy having to get up at six o'clock a.m. on a Saturday. Getting ready for my appointment at eight in the freaking morning wasn't heaven on earth.

Like *really*?

Who scheduled these appointments?

I would've scheduled me at about ten a.m.

Goodness!

It was Saturday for crying out loud.

Yes, I had a bit of an attitude when I woke up. On top of that I couldn't eat nothing because they might need to take some labs. I couldn't have anything on my stomach.

Now I was starving.

I couldn't eat until after surgery.

All I could eat was crushed ice.

WHATTTT!!!

How was I supposed to live off ice? They were trying to kill me! I was convinced. May I remind you that we've been sitting out here waiting for what felt like hours.

Not to mention the thirty minutes we had to wait before getting my IV put in my hand.

Bless her heart. The lady who was putting the IV in was having the hardest time getting my veins to cooperate.

I had running veins. It seemed like when my veins knew it was time to get my blood drawn or anything that involved a needle…they hid. As if they were ghosts. Like they were never there.

Anybody that knew me knew that I was not a fan of pain *WHATSOEVER!*

The Phlebotomist told me that she had some numbing spray. You better believe I had her use almost half the container to numb my arm and hand. I didn't want to feel nothing. I used to have a phobia. When I saw blood, I got light-headed. Like I was going to pass out, but over time I'd become more tolerant of it.

Once she got the IV in, everything was fine. She flushed it with this clear stuff. It smelled like chlorine from a swimming pool.

As I continued to adjust my body in my seat, which I'd done for the fiftieth time, I wish a nurse hurry up and take me to my room.

All I could think about was a LARGE Italian sausage and stuff crust pizza with extra parmesan from Pizza Hut. Six chocolate chip cookies from McDonalds and a Route 44 strawberry slushie with extra strawberries from Sonic.

As you could see, I was in between a rock and a hard place, while battling this uncomfortable chair and a craving that was out of this world.

"Um, Artavius?" said a woman pushing a wheelchair.

"Yes," I replied.

"I'm Shannon. I'm here to take you to your room and prep you for your surgery, are you ready?" she asked.

Shannon was a short Caucasian woman who was a brunette, with a perfect smile and wore heavy mascara. I jumped up so quick and grabbed my bag. "Whew! Yes, I am. Felt like we were waiting for ages," I said as I grabbed my stuff.

"I apologize for the wait. We had to make sure your room was ready and had everything set up for you," she explained.

"Oh no problem! The most important thing is you are here, and we can get this thing going. The faster this is over with the faster I can get my food," I said as I turned around and sat in the wheelchair.

Ha Ha Ha! "You're a little character, aren't you?" she said, laughing.

"You have no idea," Momma answered as she gathered her purse and swung the strap around her shoulder.

"I mean, I'm just saying. When you haven't eaten, you start acting crazy," I admitted.

"You're not yourself when you're hungry, right?" Shannon stated.

"Exactly," I said.

Finally, she pushed me towards the elevator. Wheelchair felt better than that chair in the waiting area.

"So, are you ready?" Shannon asked.

"Honestly, I'm a little nervous, but I know this is something I have to do. I'm as ready as I'm going to be," I said as we waited for the elevator.

At this point, I'd completely accepted whatever that needed to be done, had to be done. No time to turn back now.

One thing my grandmother taught me about faith was that once you pray about something, give it to God and leave it alone.

Trust that He would work it out in His time. He wouldn't put more on me than I could bare, and He puts His strongest soldiers through the toughest battles.

So instead of stressing about the situation, think about what lesson God wanted you to learn from it. Even though at this point I didn't understand what the lesson was, I knew before this was all over, I'll know by then.

Well there we were!

The sixth floor…

As the elevator doors opened, I was greeted with a panoramic view of the environment on the sixth floor. My anxiety begun to rise. Gripping both handles of my wheelchair, Shannon wheeled me from the front desk, past a few patients' rooms, in the direction of my assigned quarters.

Unsurprisingly, I was still taking it all in. This wasn't an environment you dissected in just a few seconds.

The nurses and patients were nice. They smiled. I didn't know if I smiled back or not.

However, I was freaked out a little bit because I was always terrified of hospitals. I was under the impression that people died in these places. I was not a fan of being here. I had no desire to be the next autopsy recipient.

No, ma'am!

Once we arrived at room 613, my room, I sighed. It took long enough. Memories of that dreaded waiting room was officially behind me.

My room had the basic setup: a bed, a bathroom, and a desk area by the window; the couch-like area was different. There was also a tray with a water jug on a small table and a box tv mounted on the wall.

"*Alright,* Artavius," said Shannon. "Here we are. I'm going to give you and your Mom a few minutes to get you settled in comfortably. In the meantime, we've placed two gowns on the bed for you to change into…one is to cover the front of your upper and lower body and the other is to cover your backside.

"By that time, I should be back," Shannon announced, "So I could take you down to the operating area and prep you for surgery."

"Okay, cool. Thank you," I answered, lifting myself out the wheelchair.

Shannon then left the room with the wheelchair.

I began to sort my stuff on the couch. I undressed, folded my clothes into a neat pile and changed into the hospital gowns.

Momma was talking on the phone, putting the remainder of our belongings in the closet.

Nearly ten minutes passed. I'm dressed for surgery.

Shannon came to get me and took me down to the operating area via the industrial elevator. Momma stayed in the room and notified me that she'll be there when I come back from surgery.

Once the elevator doors whisked open, Shannon and I was on the basement floor. She rolled me around corners and down halls until we reached the operating area.

First, the signature double doors with the wording 'OPERATING AREA' was a bit scary. I knew my alternative life was going to start behind those doors.

"You ready?" Shannon asked.

"Yes, I guess so." I was nervous. "I don't have much of a choice…"

"Oh, you're going to do just fine! We'll take great care of you," Shannon stated. She used her special badge to access the Operating Area.

As the metal doors opened, I felt the rush of a cool breeze collapse over my body. We proceed into the Operating Area.

Uneasy as all get out, I remained still by repetitively saying to myself, *"Stay calm. You're going to be alright! Relax, Tay."*

Shannon then pushed me in the room with the doctors who were going to perform my surgery. They introduced themselves and reminded me that I was going to do great.

Everything will be fine.

They gave me a quick overview on the placement of my lines. They also told me about other complex medical stuff they would do after my surgery to confirm its success.

After I confirmed my understanding of the process, Shannon left the room and my life altering procedure began.

Changing life as I knew it forever...

Alright, Artavius...Just lay back and relax. I'm going to put this blood pressure cuff on you so we can keep an eye on your blood pressure," said the nurse.

Once that was done. "Okay, so now I'm going to connect your IV to this machine," she said, "that will push some fluids in you. You're going to get sleepy, okay?"

I nodded.

"We also have some sleeping gas," she informed me. "What flavor would you like: bubble gum, watermelon, grape, strawberry...."

"Strawberry," I interrupted. That was my all-time favorite flavor with anything.

"Okay, strawberry coming right up" she said.

Quietly, she turned away and walked over to the doctors standing in the corner, talking. I felt and taste the fluids from the IV and I started getting sleepy.

As I laid, stretched out, on the operating table, looked up at the ceiling, a big, round light shined down on me.

I began to pray...

Dear Lord…it's me again!
I'm about to get my lines…
I ask of you to bless the hands of these doctors
and grant a successful operation.
I'm a little nervous, but I know you got me.
So, I trust in your plan! Lead the way and I will follow.
In Your name I pray…
Amen…

"Alright, Artavius. Take deep breaths for me," the doctor abruptly said. Casually, she walked over to my bedside and proceeded to place the gas mask over my nose and mouth.

I closed my eyes for a moment. This was it. No turning back. No opting out. I would say that she kind of scared me; like she came out of nowhere and put that mask over my mouth. Yeah, it kind of creeped me out.

I was glad that I at least finished my prayer, but anyways, as she put the mask on my nose and mouth, I smelled a hint of the strawberry flavor. Which was cool, but after about ten seconds…I didn't smell the strawberries anymore.

An unrecognizable smell invaded the scent of strawberry, which I later found out was the anesthesia.

With every deep breath I took, I was slowly drifting away. It felt like I was being hypnotized…

The room was slowly spinning...the doctor's voice sounded like a broken record that kept repeating her last few words *You're gonna be alright, okay...you're gonna be alright, okay? ... you're gonna be alright, okay?*

Images became blurs and ghosts...I was floating...it feels like I'm spinning on a merry-go-round...

I'm nodding and whispering, "ok...ok...ok..."

Then I was out like a light.

Total blackness...

With the time frame of two hours, my surgery was a success. Waking up to the sounds of machines beeping made me soon realize that I was in the ICU (Intensive Care Unit).

Recovering.

Gently wrapped in warm white blankets, my feather soft pillow and fuzzy footies were so comfortable and relaxing that everything that happened prior to waking up felt like a dream.

I meant, I wasn't sore or in pain. There was no pressure or nausea.

Nothing.

I was laying on my side, with covers pulled up to my ears. I was looking around the unit, observing the environment.

After about five minutes of watching, I tried to turn over on my back and that's when I felt something drag along the covers.

I was startled. I stopped in shock because I almost believed everything was a dream.

I slightly raised the covers to get a look at my chest or the area I felt a slight tug.

And that was when I saw the freshly taped and wrapped line on my right, upper chest…

"This is it, huh?" I whispered to my implanted lines. "Well, you and I will get to spend plenty of time together…"

"So, I see you met the lines, huh?" the doctor interrupted. He chuckled a little.

"Yeah…I was just introducing myself." I joked.

"Well good, because you two will spend lots of time together," he stated.

"Right, that's what I just said." I laughed.

"…That's good. How are you feeling?" he asked.

"I'm good, surprisingly," I answered.

"Surprisingly? You expected to feel differently?" he asked.

"Honestly, I did. I thought I would be sore or in pain. When I woke up, I didn't feel like I just had surgery. It felt like I took a good ole' nap" I explained.

"That's a good thing. We try to be sure to keep you guys comfortable and the pain to a minimum," he responded.

"Y'all are doing an amazing job" I suggested.

"Well, thank you! Let me get one more look at the catheter," the doctor suggested as he walked over to me and look at my lines.

I was thirteen years old. I should be doing teenage things…

But I was learning to adjust to my altered life.

Once he was done examining my lines, he asked was I feeling any pain. I was good. And it was official. I had a successful surgery.

"Okay, it looks good," said the doctor. "Since you're not having any issues post-surgery with any pain or discomfort, I'll relay the message to the other doctors.

They'll call Shannon to come and take you back to your room. You must rest before your first dialysis treatment tomorrow morning," he stated.

"Okay, thank you," I answered.

"If you have any questions…let one of your nurses know and they'll transfer the message to us," he said.

"Okay, great" I responded.

"…Well, you have a good rest of your evening and we'll come check on you in the dialysis unit tomorrow after your treatment," he said.

"Okay, well…I'll see you then," I responded.

"Take care," he said as he left my room.

"Thanks" I said.

About fifteen minutes after the doctor left, Shannon came to take me back to my room. During the entire wheelchair ride back to the sixth floor, I sat with my eyes closed.

Embracing the moment.

I tried to relax my body for the big day tomorrow.

Once we got back to my room it was quiet. Momma was gone and the room was a bit chilly…

Perfect for good sleeping.

"Well here we are," said Shannon. "We've set your bed up with warm blankets. I read on your chart that you were anemic. Is that why you requested two gowns and a heated blanket?" she asked.

"Yes, Ma'am. I get cold like this [snapped my fingers] and hot like that [snapped my fingers]. However, if you have a mixture of heat and cool air…its perfect.

"Like I tell people," I continued. "When you're cold you can always bundle up with clothing; but when you're hot you can only take off so much. It's not like we can take our skin off," I explained as I got out of the chair and into the bed.

I snuggled under the covers.

She chuckled. "Hey, I can understand that. My biggest concern is that you're comfortable," she interjected. Swiftly, she connected me back to the IV fluids and blood pressure cuff.

"Thank you," I said.

I tried to get adjusted and comfortable in bed.

"You're welcome. Now before I leave…I want to let you know a few things. This here is your morphine fluids. You only use it when you're in pain. To activate it, you would push this button and it'll release a dose through your IV okay?

"Alright, next thing," she continued. "This machine is set to take your blood pressure every fifteen to thirty minutes. I'm about to get off in the next ten minutes. Ms. Push Pam is your scheduled nurse and she will take great care of you overnight…

"You're going to love her… *Sweet* lady," she concluded.

"Push Pam? Is that *really* her name or is it like a nickname? Does she push people or something?" I interrupted.

Hahahahaaa!

"No, that's her *real* name and no she *doesn't* push people." She was laughing. "She'll be here with you overnight. I'll be back at seven in the morning to take you down to the dialysis unit for your first treatment."

"Okay. Thank you and see you tomorrow," I said.

"You have a good rest of your evening," she said.

"I'm going to try, hopefully. I could sleep the rest of the night," I responded.

"Okay, oh and the remote to turn on the TV is over here on the side. If you need anything press the nurse button on the remote and someone at the front desk will answer," Shannon said as she showed me the remote.

"Oh, okay…cool. Thank you," I said.

"You're welcome…Well, let me go. I'll see you bright and early tomorrow," she said.

"Okay" I responded.

"Alright, see you later," she said as she walked towards the door.

"See ya," I said and waved.

The room door closed behind her…

"Well, I guess this is it…in less than twelve hours I will start the first day of I don't know *how* long," I said amongst myself.

As I laid there, pondering over my imposing first day of treatment, I found myself falling deep into my thoughts.

I was overthinking the entire situation. I was mentally freaking out.

My first night in the hospital was everything but peaceful.

I was tossing and turning, getting used to my lines, the machine beeping, nurses coming in and out the room taking my blood pressure and temperature…

Finally, I got a good nod in before drifting to sleep.

I didn't know who said that you get to rest while you're in the hospital…

They lied.

Chapter 6:

First Day in Hell's Playground

IT was about 5:30 a.m. and I was laying on my right side, gazing out the sixth floor window as I tried yet again to drift off into some kind of a sleep. Fifteen minutes later…I was still just lying there.

Come on now, Tay. You need to try and rest.

You already know it's going to be a long day once dialysis start.

You should clear your mind and quit freaking out over things you haven't experience yet.

You are going to be just fine.

God got you, remember. Now get some rest…

I tried to clear my head of the traumatic thoughts and dreams I created for my first day of dialysis.

In my dream, my mind created dialysis as a "special place" that was housed by this devil-like figure. It just kept playing over and over in my head. He came around the unit collecting all the patients' blood that'd been drained by these big machines.

Then I woke up, and at this point I was too spooked to go back to sleep…

I didn't want to continue in that dream in what felt like hell. I got to stop reading those Goosebumps books.

Knock at the door. "Good morning!" Shannon announced as she came in and turned the lights on. My instant moans and groans filled my ears. I covered my head with the covers with an attitude. As soon as I finally fell asleep, boom! Lights on!

Was this a trick? I didn't want to rise and shine! I wanted SLEEP! April Fool's, right? *Ughhh*!

I bet she slept like a baby. Look at her. Came in my space all smiling and rested. As for me. I couldn't sleep. I had nightmares. And now that I found sleep, I was awakened for a day I wasn't looking forward to.

Dialysis…

"Wakey-Wakey! Today's the big day!"

Ughhh!

"It's now seven o'clock," she said, "and we got to have you down in the dialysis unit by eight o'clock."

"Go away! I didn't want to let go of this much needed sleep!" I said in my head.

"Come on Tay," Momma said a bit sternly. "Get up. You got to get ready." She stood up and stretched.

"Okay, so I'm going to let you get dressed and I'll be back around 7:30 so we can all head down together," Shannon suggested.

"Alright, thank you," Momma said. She walked over to the closet to get her bag out.

At this point I was a bit aggravated, which was nothing new when I'd been awakened from my sleep. However, this time I was not just mad because I'd been bothered from my slumber, but because after battling horrible dreams and nerves, I finally was sleeping peacefully for the first time the whole night.

Not to mention how many times my machines kept beeping and the nurse constantly came in and out the room.

"Alright now, Tay! Come on, get up! You already know what you got to do so quit playing," Momma said. She walked around the bed to the bathroom.

So, by this time I was already over the situation and this first day of treatment. I then slowly, but surely, got up and got dressed.

First, I turned over on my back, waited a few seconds to gather my thoughts, then I removed my covers.

I waited for a few seconds to prepare myself for this day, this process, then I raised up and turned to my left. My feet hung off the side of the bed, then I got up and got myself together for treatment.

Now about twenty minutes passed, and I was ready. I was sitting on the couch, waiting for Shannon.

Momma came out of the bathroom, dressed and ready.

"Well, I'm about to go to the house and get some more clothes," she told me. "By the time I get back you should be done with your treatment…You scared?" she asked.

"I'm good; I'll be alright" I lied, knowing I was terrified.

"Okay, well…I'll see you later. Text me," she said and grabbed her purse.

She was headed towards the door.

"Okay, I will," I responded…

As she left.

About two minutes after Momma left, Shannon came in with the wheelchair. "Alright! You're all set and ready to head down? she asked.

"Yep! let's do this!" I said with confidence, surprisingly, as I got off the couch and sat in the wheelchair.

"I talked to your mother as she was leaving. She said she'll be back after your treatment and to call her if we need anything," she said.

"Yeah, okay…she told me to text her," I responded.

"Okay, great! Well, let's head down. I believe if everything goes well after treatment and you're feeling okay, they'll let you go home," she said as she rolled me out the room.

The whole ride from my room to the dialysis unit was quiet. All I could think about was the scary dreams I kept having about my first day of treatment. I was praying and trying to stay positive on this journey to the dialysis unit. After about five minutes that felt like a good ten minutes in my head, we finally made it to the door that read:

Dialysis Unit

We're here," she said. She reached to open the door to push me in. As soon as the doors opened my heart stopped. Everything started going in slow motion. Machines beeped repetitiously, there was loud screaming; nurses talked with patients and family while other nurses took notes of some patients' charts…

A few people stared at me; a few others were trying to see who that was coming through the door, being nosey.

"Good Morning! You must be Artavius?" the nurse at the front desk asked.

"Yes, ma'am" I responded.

"We've been looking forward to meeting you. Welcome to the dialysis unit. My name is Deloris and I'll be helping get you all set up for your first treatment, okay?

"Alright," Deloris went on, "so…if you could go ahead, get up here on this scale…we can get a starting weight on you."

She reached her hand out to help me out of the wheelchair and onto the scale.

"Alright. I'm going to head back upstairs. Deloris, can you call me when he's about done with treatment."

"I sure will," Deloris answered.

"I need time to finish what I'm doing. I'll head down here to pick him up and take him back to the room."

Deloris smiled and nodded.

"*Thanks*. See you in a few hours, Artavius," Shannon said. She walked backwards with the wheelchair and headed out the door.

I stepped on the scale to see how much I weighed. When I looked down to see how much the scale said I weighed it was in a different format, it was in kilograms instead of pounds.

"*Good*. Now that we have a starting weight for you, you can meet me in that room over there." She pointed at it. "You got your own room and not one that's separated by a curtain."

"I'll be right back" I said.

I grabbed the gowns and started walking to the restroom.

It took Deloris about three minutes to finish my paperwork and get back to the room where my first treatment would be. One thing I noticed right off the back from coming into that room. It was so cold! Mind you…I was anemic. Therefore, I got cold and hot easily. To me it felt like I was getting a taste of Antarctica with a side of Alaska's blizzard.

"Jesus, its cold in here!" I said as I entered the room and put my clothes in a chair by the door.

"Yeah…it is a lil' bit chilly in here," she agreed.

"A lil' bit? It's a lot bit chilly. Feels like Alaska in here," I said. I shivered hard. It looked like I was doing the old dance called the Harlem shake.

"Hahaha! you're so silly. You remind me of one of our other nurses here. Ms. Violet. She's silly, too. You'll love her. I brought some blankets for you. We can even warm them up if you want," she suggested.

"These will do alright for now" I said.

I sat in the reclining chair, snuggled under the two thick white blankets and tried to get comfy.

"Great. Let's get started. Are you ready?" she asked.

"Yeah" I said.

I sat back in the reclining chair and watched Deloris work.

As I sat and watched her, she reached beside the machine and grabbed two clear cords. One with a blue clamp and the other with a red clamp.

"Deloris…what are those for?" I asked.

She sat the cords across the chair and in my lap.

"These are going to be connected to your dialysis catheter or your lines," she answered.

"What lines?" I acted ignorant and confused to get her to explain it more.

"The ones you have on your chest," she said. "Lines is just another word people use for the catheter. See, look." She removed the tape from the catheter that was surgically put in me for dialysis purposes.

Once she completely removed the tape and dressing, she revealed two other clear cords, parallel to the ones she placed in my lap; but shorter.

"The shorter cords…they're color coordinated with the red and blue clamps of the longer ones. So, this is where the machine takes all the blood," I said fascinatedly.

"Yes! *Good guess!* The dialysis catheter has two lumens which are the two clear cords. One is called the venous and the other one is the arterial. So how it works is, the line with the red clamp, the arterial lumen, is the one that pulls the blood out of the body. From there, it goes into the machine.

"The machine filters or cleanses the blood. Once it goes through all of that, it goes back into the body via the line with the blue clamp--the venous lumen," she further explained.

She pointed to a trail directing the movements of blood and how it moved from me, through the machine, and back into me.

"Oh, okay. Pretty simple." I nodded in understanding.

"Yeah…you're going to be on the machine for three hours, three days a week," she stated.

"I remember my doctors saying that. I have a question. What is that smell?" I asked, confused. "It smells like pool water and chlorine."

She cackled. "Yeah…the two containers down here on the side of the machine has some chlorine in it. Just as chlorine is used to clean swimming pools, rid them of all the bacteria, it's used to clean the blood as well.

"The containers are called 'Dialysate'," she continued. "It's also referred to as 'dialysis fluid,' 'dialysis solution' or 'bath'. It is a solution of pure water, electrolytes and salts, such as bicarbonate and sodium.

"The purpose of it is to pull all the toxins and bad stuff from the blood before it goes back into your body," she said in conclusion.

"Really? I would've never guessed that," I responded.

"Now, it's not the exact chlorine solution found in swimming pools, but the dialysate has a type of chlorine in it.

"We get a lot of new patients. They ask the same questions. They found out there's chlorine in the solution and they all make funny faces and say '*CHLORINE!*' Like pool water chlorine? It's hilarious" she mentioned.

I laughed. "I bet! So how long do a person tend to be on dialysis before they get a new kidney?" I asked.

"It's different for each patient. It depends on how long it takes for a match to come in from a living or deceased donor, and if it's that patient's turn on the waiting list," she explained.

"Waiting list? Why does that sound like the line is forever long and we have to wait until infinity and beyond before we get to the front," I stated.

"Well, yeah. There's quite a few thousand people on the list," she hinted.

"What's a few thousand? Like three or four thousand?" I continued to ask.

A hearty chuckle. "*No.* I don't know the *exact* number as of now, but I know it's over eighty thousand people," she assumed.

"*EIGHTY THOUSAND!?* You can't put the word 'few' in front of eighty thousand. *THAT'S A LOT!*" I was in shock.

"Yeah, it *is* a lot. That's why we try to encourage people to become organ donors. Spread the word. A single person can save up to eight lives with their organs; and could help enhance the lives of up to fifty people with their tissues," she explained.

"Wow! I did not know that. So, what's the longest you've witnessed or heard about someone being on dialysis?" I asked out of curiosity.

"If I'm not mistaken…I believe I personally know someone who gets treatment and has been getting it for about twenty plus years; but there are some cases where some patients have been on dialysis the rest of their lives.

"…But again, it's different with each patient. Some are on dialysis for twenty plus years; then some are on here a year or less," she continued to explain.

"Twenty plus? Lord have mercy! That is my entire life plus some! Jesus! I'm just thirteen! I don't turn fourteen 'til next month. Lord!" I acted out jokingly.

"You're so silly," she said, laughing.

"Who has been here, or got treatment the longest?" I asked.

"We have a patient, name Jessica, next door on the other side of this wall here; she's been here with us for about ten years now," she said.

"Ten years! Oh, Lord! I'm going to be here forever!" I said in sorrow.

"No! Everybody's time is not the same. Some people may be on the machine just a year before getting a transplant or maybe a few months; like I said…it's different for each patient," she clarified.

"Oh, okay. Good. I hope and pray I get mine early. I'm finally about to go to high school. I want to be able to participate in stuff. You know…what teenagers do," I said, relieved.

"Yeah, I understand. Being on dialysis can really change a person; limit them on things they use to be able to do. But once they receive the kidney or organ transplant, they're able to participate in more activities and things of that nature," she explained.

"Man, that's crazy! Well I hope I can get my transplant fast and early so I can continue with my life," I said.

"Yeah, me, too…but it'll be over before you know it. So, let's go ahead and get you hooked up to the machine so we can begin your first treatment," she said.

She picked up the dialysis catheters she laid across my lap earlier.

She expertly connected the catheters from the machine to the ones that were parallel to the catheters implanted in my chest.

She tapped some buttons on the touch screen of the machine.

Before I knew it, I watched as the blood from my body flowed smoothly through the clear line. It was filtered by the machine and flowed back into my body through the line. Just like Deloris explained earlier.

"Alright, you're all set! Everything is good for three hours. Before I go, do you need anything? If not, I'll be checking in on you and the machine periodically," she said.

"No, I'm fine at the moment…thank you," I said and adjusted myself in the reclining chair. I was trying to get comfortable.

"Alright, well just let me know if you need anything. The other nurses and I are right outside your door at the desk," she informed me.

"Okay, thanks." I smiled.

"No problem…You want me to turn the light off and close the door?" she asked.

"Yes, please," I answered. I pulled the cover up to my chin.

"Alright," she said and turned the light off. Once she closed the glass door, she backed out of the room.

A deep exhale escaped my lips…

Well, here I am...having my first dialysis treatment. As I glanced up at the machine, I spoke to my Heavenly Father. "Lord, I don't know Your plan or what You have in stored for me on this journey, but I trust You. I know You won't leave me...You wouldn't put more on me than I could bare...

All I ask is that You bless me with patience. I've heard about a few timelines for some of the patients waiting for a kidney transplant and it scared me. I couldn't imagine being on this machine three days a week, for three-hour treatments, for ten years.

"I'm not rushing You, God...but, *please,* can I get the shortest time on dialysis? I'm not saying that my situation is better than anyone else, but I really feel like You anointed a calling over my life to help others...if I'm on dialysis I don't think I could work at my full potential.

But I know, whatever You choose to do, it'll be the best decision...so I thank You in advance. I guess I'll try to get some sleep now. I got three hours of treatment and the more I look at the clock the slower I feel like it's going."

After my heart to heart with God, amongst myself, I soon leaned over towards the machine to get comfortable enough to relax...

And drifted to sleep.

THREE HOURS LATER...

"Artavius...Artavius!" I heard Deloris call my name as I awakened from the overhead light coming on and the machine beeping.

"Yes…" I said. My head was underneath the covers.

"Time to wake up. Your first treatment is done," she said as she walked to the machine, to stop the beeping.

"Already? It feels like I just got here," I replied, still under the covers. I instantly hated that I had to get up from my comfortable position.

"Yes sir. It's been three hours. By the way… your doctors are here to speak with you before you leave," she informed.

She continued to press buttons on the machine. "Alright, come on…! You got to sit up for me so I can unhook you from the machine," she continued pleasantly as she gently removed the cover from over my head.

"Okay, okay!" I retorted. "I'm up! I was sleeping so good. That lil' piece of a nap was pretty good! I may have to finish that when I get back to the room," I went on jokingly as Deloris removed and unscrewed the catheters from my *surgical* catheters.

"Lil piece of a nap?" Her laugh was sharp. "Boy, you are so silly!"

"Good morning, Artavius!" The doctor's said in harmony as they entered the area and created a semi-circle around me.

"Oop…oh okay. Uhh…good morning," I said. "Y'all deep this morning, aren't you? I like the lil prayer circle y'all got going! *That's* cute," I continued, joking with doctors.

Hahahahaha! The doctors and Deloris laughed.

"You're a quite a character huh?" one of the doctors said as he continued to laugh.

"Yes, he is! He's been cracking me up all morning," Deloris responded.

"Well that's good," one of the doctors stated. "Well, Artavius. I'm here with the dialysis team on behalf of Dr. Ault to check in with you…to see how your first dialysis treatment went."

"Well so far, so good I guess," I answered. "It wasn't as bad as I thought it would be."

"Good, good. Um, do you feel woozy or light-headed?" the doctor asked.

"At the moment no, but I'm sure I'll find out really quick when I stand up huh," I said jokingly.

"Right, okay what about feeling any nausea or cramps" the doctor continued.

"My stomach hurt a little, but I'm sure it's because I'm hungry," I suggested.

"Yeah, okay…Be sure to put something on your stomach before taking your medication. You don't want to take them on an empty stomach," the doctor added.

"Yes, I know. Momma told me about that," I responded.

"Alright, Artavius. Do you have any questions for us or Dr. Ault before we go?" the doctor asked.

"No Sir, thank y'all so much," I answered with a smile.

"Okay, well you have a great rest of your day. Take it easy and don't forget to eat something as soon as you leave," the doctor said.

"Oh, trust me I won't forget to eat; that's one thing I don't miss. I'm going to text my momma to bring me some Subway as soon as I get back to my room," I said happily.

"Really, that sounds good. What do you get from Subway?" One of the other doctors asked.

"Well I'm glad you asked. I get a footlong oven-roasted chicken breast on nine grain honey oat bread, *lightly* toasted. I don't want my bread burnt or hard. As for the toppings, I get lettuce, three tomatoes, mayo, salt and pepper.

I was warming to the subject of food.

I was famished. "Then I'll get three chocolate chip cookies, spicy nacho cheese Doritos and a Sprite with light ice. When I tell you...*BLESS MY SOUL*! Taste like Jesus Christ Himself made that! *Oooweeee*! *THANK YA!*"

I was a bit animated as I lifted my hands in praise.

I was imagining how I would feel after eating my food.

"You eat all of that by yourself?" the woman doctor asked, amused...

"Girl, *yeah*! I don't believe in sharing my food. *No ma'am!* Un-uh, that's against my religion right there. Don't let my small frame fool you...I can eat!" I said jokingly. I shook my head and brought my hands back down.

"Really? Not even a piece for someone to sample to see if they like it before ordering one?" she responded.

"Girl, *nah*! This isn't Sam's...a place where you sample everything in the store. You better get in line and *Get Your Own!* Like the snacks Cheez-It slogan say, *Get Your Own Box* – I tell 'em, *Get Your Own Sandwich*," I humored.

The doctors erupted into hearty chuckles.

"*O-M-G! You* are hilarious! I got to tell my friends that one," the female doctor responded.

"See, I told y'all. He's been going all morning," Deloris interrupted.

"We see!" the female doctor agreed. "Now remember, don't consume too much salt or too many tomatoes or anything high in phosphorus," the male doctor added.

"Yeah I know. That's why I specifically say three, because they'll put six or seven on your sandwich. That'll have my blood pressure sky high. I be on it when someone makes my food. I know exactly how I want my stuff," I stated.

"Good…Well, let us get going. You have a great rest of your morning. I'm sure you'll see us around," the male doctor said, as he and the rest of the team followed him out of the room.

"Alright, thank y'all. Have a good one" I said.

I smiled and waved.

"Alright, now…stand up for me so we can take your pressure and you're all done. Then you can get dressed and I'll call Shannon so she can come get you," Deloris stated.

"Okay…I'm sholl hungry," I said as I started to rock and get out the reclining chair. Was "sholl" even a word. I smiled.

"Whew…I'm getting old," I continued to joke as I struggled getting out of the chair.

"Oh, boy…hush. You're barely a teenager. Talking 'bout you're old. Come on here and take this blood pressure," she said and laughed.

Haahaahaha! "I sholl feel like it. The chair doesn't want to let me go," I said, and I stood up.

"It doesn't want you to go, huh?" she added.

"*Right*! That little piece of a nap was good, too. I got to finish that nap once I finish eating and being blessed from that Subway sandwich. Hopefully they discharge me today so I can go home and lay in my bed tonight instead of the hospital bed," I said, waiting for her to finish taking my blood pressure.

"Boy you are so silly. Okay, now your pressure is good. You can go change back into your clothes, with your silly self," she said. She took the blood pressure cuff off my arm.

"I mean, *hey*! I'm just saying…get you one of those Jesus sandwiches and receive that BLESSING, GIRL!" I was on a roll.

"Artavius go put your clothes on…" she said. She shook her head and laughed.

"Yes, Ma'am!" I grabbed my clothes, laughing as I headed to the rest room to change into my street clothes.

Later, after getting dressed, I joked around with the other nurses. I met Jessica and a few other patients, and we laughed until Shannon came down to take me back to my room.

Once I got back to my room, I found out everything was good, but my doctor wanted to keep me for one more night; just to see how my body reacted after my first dialysis treatment.

I was discharged the next day around noon. I had my momma stop by Subway again so I can get me one of those soul blessing Jesus sandwiches.

My first treatment wasn't so bad.

I probably could do this for a lil bit, but only time would tell…

CHAPTER 7:

THE DEVIL THOUGHT HE HAD ME

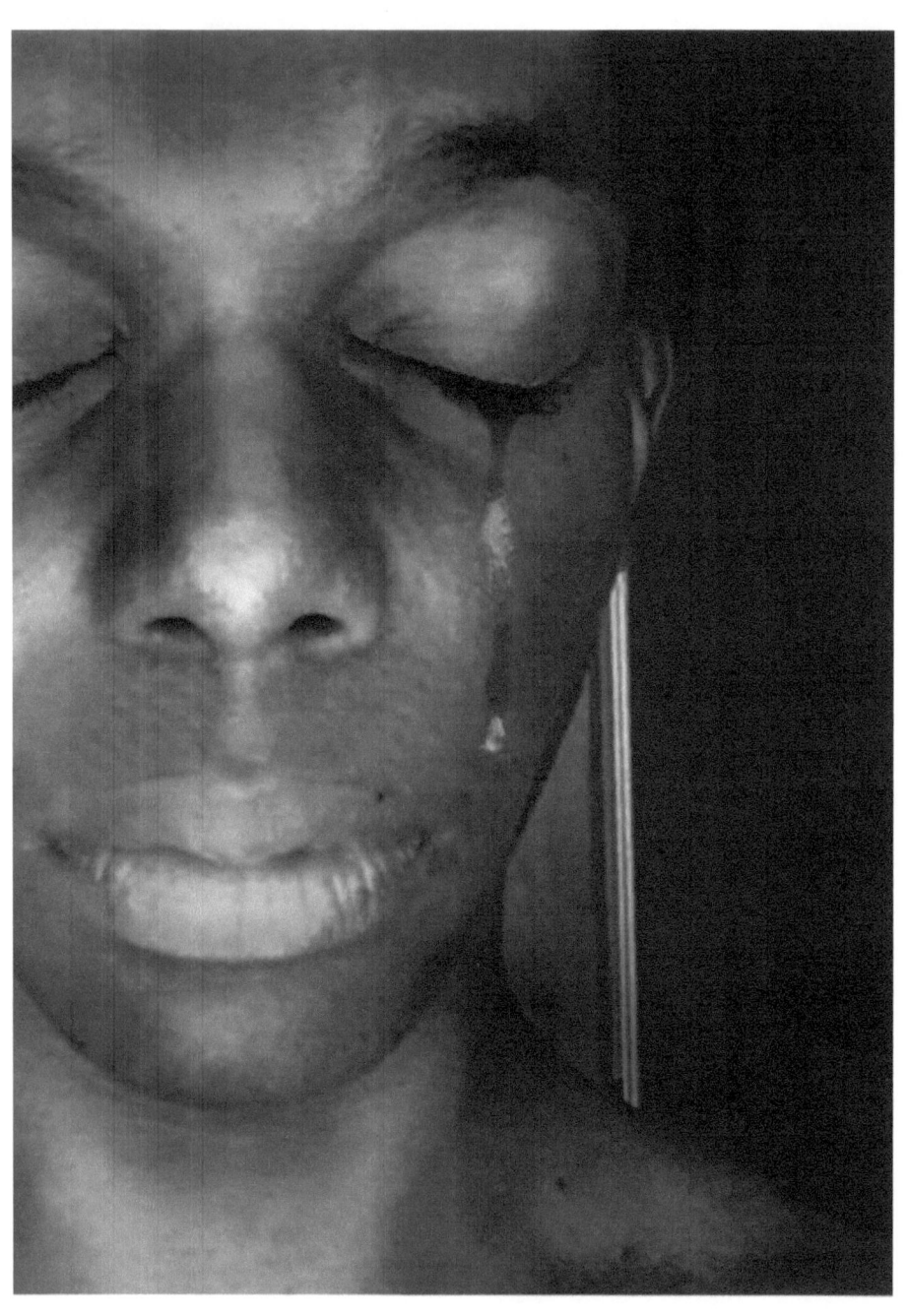

82 BECOMING A LIVING TESTIMONY

FIFTEEN MONTHS LATER...

Before I realized it, fifteen months drifted on by since I started dialysis treatment. It was April 6, 2005. I was fifteen years old. Where did the time go...? *Lately,* things hadn't been looking too good for me. I'd become overwhelmed, weak and almost always *too* tired to do anything. Not to mention that I was a high schooler. A freshman at that. I often had mood swings. All I had energy for was laying down and attempting to rest.

Visits to the hospital for treatment went from fun and talkative mornings, to quiet, aggravated and constant pain spells. Just when I felt that matters couldn't get any worse, they did!

I'd never forget one of those disquieting days of treatment. I was about halfway through my treatment when I got an unexpected visit from my primary care doctor, Dr. Ault during my treatment.

Knock, Knock...!

"Good Morning, Artavius...How are you?" Dr Ault greeted as she walked into my room.

"Hey, I'm alright. I can't complain," I said softly.

I was curled up in a ball under the heated blanket.

"It's a little chilly in here," she started, "but I was dropping by to talk to you for a minute. How have things been?" she asked.

She squatted alongside my reclining chair so she could be eye level with me.

"I mean, it's going...it's a bit rough, but I'm hanging in there..."

"I see. You're such a fighter. It's admiring to see such a small guy with so much power and faith," she replied.

"Well, honestly, I don't have a choice but to be strong" I responded. I sat up.

"And it's so inspiring. I hope it rubs off on some of the other patients in the unit; they all love you and your fun personality" she continued.

"Thank you. I appreciate that," I replied with a smirk on my face.

"Oh, you're more than welcome…but the *other* reason why I'm here is to let you know what's going on with your line," she admitted.

"Okay, because my line has been acting crazy. It works when it wants to work," I told her.

"Exactly. So, what that tells us is that your catheter is blowing out and needs to be replaced."

When I heard her say that my heart dropped to my stomach. Not only was I dealing with stress from school, trying to keep up in class, battling bouts of weakness from the extra fluids that had to be taken out of my body; now I have to go through surgery again to get a new dialysis catheter. I just knew my blood pressure went up about twenty points after hearing this news.

"So…they have to take this one out and put in another one?" I asked sadly.

"I'm afraid so. Where do you want us to place the new line? On the left side of your chest, your arm or stomach?" she asked me.

"It can't go back in the same spot?" I asked in confusion.

"No. *That* location has been used and we can't reuse that same spot," she answered.

"Ughhh…okay, uhh…I definitely don't want it in my stomach. My mom had her line in her arm, and it got her arm looking weird and bruised up.

Plus, I touched it one time and it was vibrating. That freaked me out so *no ma'am!* I don't want that. Plus, I have small arms. That won't be a good look either." I voiced my opinion.'

"Okay, well we can defiantly put it on the other side of your chest. No problem. I just wanted to give you your options," she responded.

"Thank you. I hate to have another scar on my body, but I guess I don't have much of a choice, huh?" I asked.

"Not much, because we have to create another site where we can do your treatment. We scheduled your surgery for tomorrow morning. Once you finish your treatment today, we're going to admit you in the hospital and get you all set up for surgery. If all is well after surgery, we might let you leave Sunday," she said.

In my head, I was like, *dang!* I was looking forward to chilling this weekend. I could possibly catch up on some sleep. I knew I wasn't going to get no type of rest, sleep, nap, wink or nod in the hospital.

Assigned nurses only come in your room every ten to fifteen minutes to check your temperature and blood pressure; just to see if anything changed.

Now I knew my blood pressure was going to be high because this was pissing me off and ruined my weekend plans.

"Oh--*tomorrow*, okay. Y'all don't waste no time. huh?" I said in shock.

"Well we try to fix it as soon as we can so when you come back for treatment Monday, you'll be all set and ready to go," she responded.

"Yeah I see." I was still in a state of shock.

"Okay, well…I guess I'll go fill out the rest of your paperwork so you can be admitted into the hospital and I'll see you either Saturday or Sunday to check on you and the new line," she stated.

"Do you need anything from me or one of the nurses right now?" she continued.

"No, ma'am, I'm fine thank you" I responded.

"Alright then. I'll see you this weekend after surgery," she said as she stood up from the squatting position.

"Have a great rest of your day," she continued. She looked back at me and smiled before opening the door.

"You, *too*" I said with a slight smirk on my face.

The door closed.

She was gone…

Once Dr. Ault left, I almost instantly sunk into a deep depression…filled with regret. Impulsively, I automatically blamed myself. I felt guilty. I was apologetic to myself for not taking care of my lines. There was undue pressure and weight put on me…I honestly didn't know what to do…

But cry…

Everything seemed to be going wrong. All at the same time.

And like clockwork, the overflow of negative thoughts begun to surface.

If only I stuck to the diet the nurses provided; if only I drank more water; if only I got more sleep; if only I didn't wait until the last minute to do stuff; if only I cared a bit more; if only I was more appreciative…

Then NONE of this would've happened to me.

I brought this pain on myself. *Therefore*, I must suffer the consequences.

Little did I know, at the time, that the devil got into my head and made me believe this was all my fault. And all my doing; rather than believe what my grandmother used to always tell me.

In retrospect, her words filtered into my brain.

"You're on a journey," she once said. *"And right now, you're going through the storm. Keep your head up and focus on God. He will guide you through. Don't allow the enemy in and have you all crazy in the head.*

"The Lord has a plan and purpose for all of us," she continued. *"Some things may seem unfair, but just trust Him and the journey. He's doing it for a reason! Sooner or later it'll make sense.*

"Just continue to walk with God. He won't put more on you then you can bare."

Immediately, I snapped out of those self-destructing thoughts and began to pray.

"Dear Lord...

Can you please help me? I'm in between a rock and a hard place. I honestly don't know if I should cry, be mad or jump off a bridge. I mean...everything is going wrong!

So here I am Lord...Calling out Your name for help and guidance. I know that I'm supposed to trust in You and the journey, but, Lord, it's hard sometimes.

I get lost in my head so much. I battle my thoughts and emotions daily. I just don't know what to do or believe anymore.

So, if You can please help me with this, I will make a deal with you. If you can get me through my ordeal, I promise I will do everything in my power to share my story. My testimony. To help as many people as You allow me to help.

I just can't be on dialysis forever. Please help me. I PROMISE once I get through this and receive my new kidney, I will make it my mission to inspire others along my journey and those who battle kidney disease.

Any other purpose my story, gift, talents or skills serve let Your Will be done. I will comply...

You have my word. I pinky promise..."

Before I could even finish my prayer, I felt a strong shiver and release of heat from my body. Amongst the shivers, the voices in my head was silenced.

It was finally quiet.

I felt a sense of vindication. I *knew* that was the Lord!

He heard my cry.

"God?"

Silence.

"Thank you!"

I knew that He heard me! I could literally feel His presence! The warm sensation that engulfed me after my prayer was confirmation.

Feeling blessed, I sat there in peace and quiet. I was grateful. I leaned back in the reclining chair for the rest of my treatment. My door opened. "Tay-Tay?" Ms. Violet said as she entered the room.

"Yes ma'am. I'm woke," I replied.

"Your treatment is over for the day. How are you feeling?" she asked after turning the overhead lights on.

"*Blessed!*" I said with a smile on my face.

"Well alrighty then. There goes that beautiful smile! I haven't seen you smile in a lil' minute. You've been looking a bit down lately. Is everything's okay?" she asked in concern.

"I'm fine now; but honestly…it's been a lot going on in my life. Dealing with dialysis, always feeling weak after treatments, try'na keep up in school, all my friends wanting to know what's wrong with me…

"Why I'm always at the hospital," I went on, "and don't have time to hang out anymore. Then on top of all *that*, Dr. Ault just told me my line has blown out and I got to get another one put in this weekend…

"…Which means that I have to be in the hospital all weekend. I planned on being at home, getting my rest because we all know I don't get to rest in the hospital," I further explained.

"Yeah…that's what she was just telling me a minute ago," she said.

"Right! Now that's *another weekend* in the hospital, and *another* few days I can't hang out with my friends. I haven't told them what's going on. I don't want everybody in my business. I already know they're not going to understand at all.

"As soon as they find out that I have kidney disease they're going to think it's contagious," I assumed. "They'll think I'm dying. They might not hang out with me anymore. I don't want to lose the few friends I have. If I do, then who am I going to talk to?" I said sadly.

"Well…you can talk to me!" she joked.

I laughed. "Yeah, I know…but outside of here though."

"I can give you my number and you can call me whenever you feel like talking," she generously offered. "It ain't no problem. You know that."

"Thank you, Ms. Violet. I really appreciate it. Other than that, I've just been trying to keep it together and juggle everything," I confessed.

"Well, baby, you don't want to worry yourself sick. Don't shut yourself out from everybody when you have people here willing to help you. People that love and care about you. You don't have to tackle all of this on your own. And I'm sure you know that…

"I'm gonna tell ya' one thing I've learned over the years. Friends come and go. If they don't accept you for who you are and what you bring to the table, then they aren't really your friends," she said.

"Yeah, I know. You sound just like my grandma. She always tells me that I'm doing too much, slow down, take some time off and get myself together and stop worrying about what others think of me. At the end of every day…if you're happy with the person you see in the mirror, the hell with everybody else and their opinions!"

"Well she's definitely right about that," she agreed.

"I'm working on it. I'm a work in progress," I said.

"Yeah we all are baby," she continued to agree.

"It's just a lot. I honestly just want a break from it all. Relax a little bit and get my mind right. Then come back strong and equipped and tackle everything heads on," I said wishful thinking.

"Well, speaking of break, what about signing up for Camp Okawehna this year. You missed it last year. Have you seen the pictures? Everybody had a blast! I think you should go this year. It's the perfect timing for you. Plus, I'll be there again this year, so you know it's going to be a load of fun." She was amped.

"They did look like they had a bunch of fun. I was just nervous last year. I was getting comfortable and coping with the whole dialysis thing. I wasn't too sure going out of town for a whole week with people I barely knew was plausible. Not being mean or anything, but I didn't know y'all like that."

"But you know us now." She laughed.

"I know, right!" I agreed, laughing.

"So, you can come and get on that bus and go have some fun with the other kidney patients around the world. Look at it like a vacation away from everything. You said you wanted a break. Well here you go! It's just a week--not to short or too long. Just enough time to clear your head.

"When it's over you'll be all refreshed and ready to handle the stuff that you mentioned you wanted to take care of...so *boom*, problem solved," she explained, smiling.

"Alright now! You better get me together!" I laughed.

"I'm just saying. You are way too young to be stressed out like you are. You have such a beautiful spirit. Don't allow the challenges and people in this world to get you down. You have so much going for you. You're young! Go out and have fun!" she suggested. "Make new friends and experience new things. You're gonna love it!"

"Alright, alright I'll do it. I'll talk to my grandma about it. I got to get this school stuff situated and catch up with everything because I'm behind like crazy," I explained.

"Speaking of school, have you ever thought about home school? The school will send a teacher to the house and work with you on the classwork just as if you were going to class" she mentioned.

"No. I haven't honestly. I just know my mom not going to let that happen. She doesn't like random people in her house," I said, laughing.

"Well if she sees that you're behind in school and this option would help you academically, I don't see why she wouldn't allow it," she said.

"I don't know, Ms. Violet, that's my mama for you," I said as I shrugged my shoulders.

"Well, I'm going to speak with Dr. Ault and see if we can work that out for you," she said as she finished disconnecting me from the machine.

"Okay, thank you. Can I also get the paperwork for Camp so I can fill that out, too?" I asked.

"You sure can! I'll give it to you before you leave today," she said.

"Thank you…" I sighed.

"Oh, you're welcome, Sweetie," she said as she continued pressing buttons on the machine.

From that moment, believe it or not, everything felt like it was on the up and up for me. For the first time in a while I wasn't feeling too dizzy or weak after treatment. I chatted with some of the other patients that were still there to see if they were going to Camp this year. I was telling them that I was thinking about going.

The other nurses--Ms. Deloris and Ms. Sherry--were happy to finally see me back to smiling and socializing with everybody.

It felt good to be around a lot of positive energy for a change.

Later on, I was admitted into the hospital…

The following day I had my surgery.

It was a success.

Everything worked out fine…

I was patched up and ready for treatment with my new line Monday morning.

That weekend, for me. was full of positive energy and blessings.

I couldn't do nothing but thank God because He's surely the reason and gets all the glory.

I had my late-night shift nurse, Ms. Push Pam, again. She wasn't bad at all.

I was up late chatting with her; having fun; making everybody laugh; acting silly.

So, it was a good weekend after all.

I was excited to keep all the positive energy and see what happened next...

CHAPTER 8

A Week of Stress Therapy

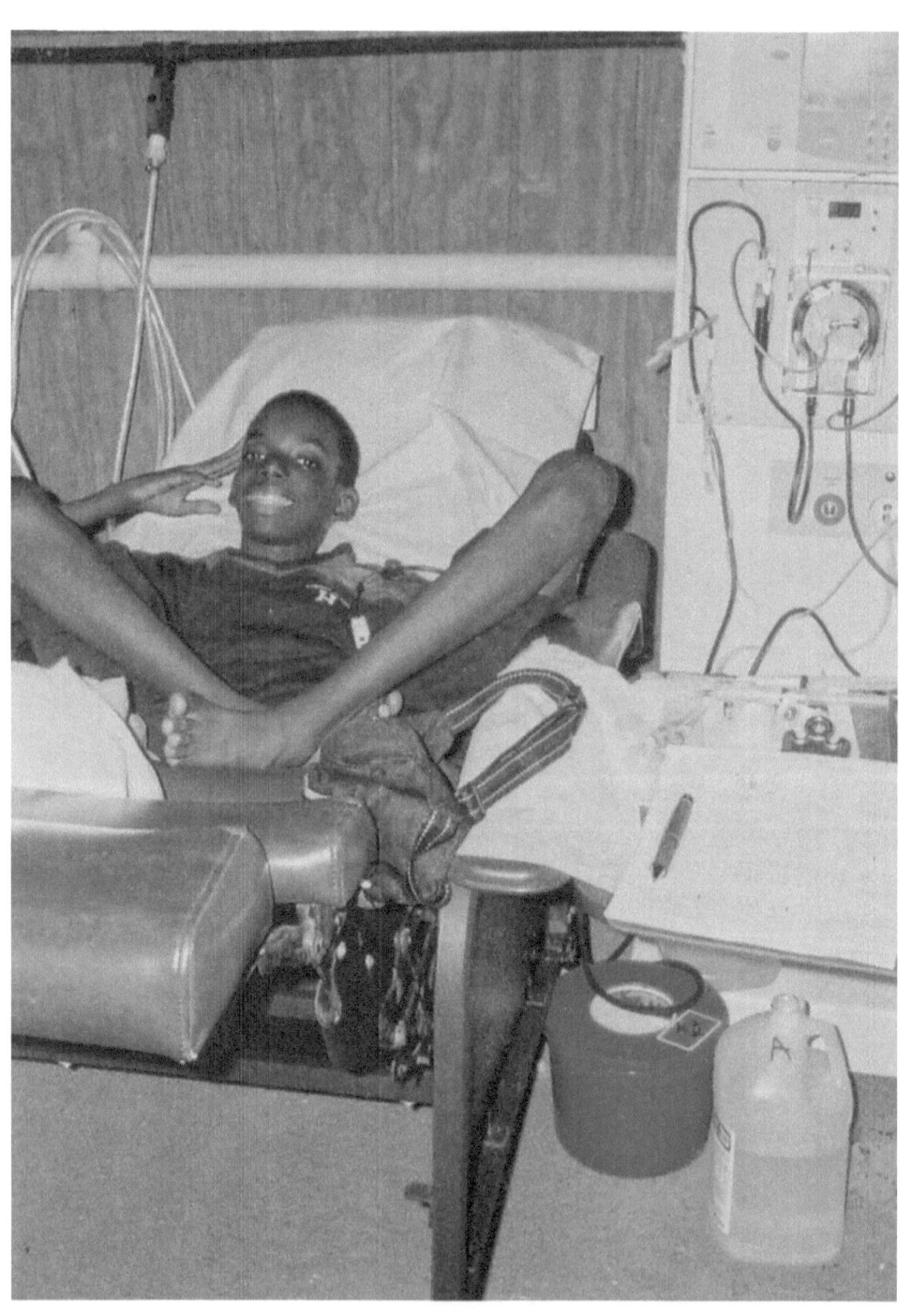

The time was here! June finally arrived. Everything so far had been great and going smoothly. Since my prayer and promise to God, things for the most part had been on the upside for me. I was able to finish my first year as a high schooler successfully. I didn't have straight A's, but my grades were good enough to get me through the first year. The nurses and my doctors communicated with both my mother and the school administration to get me approved to be home schooled for my first semester as a tenth grader.

A sophomore…

So, I was so excited about that. I was still stressed a little bit, but nowhere near the stress levels that I used to be.

I was appreciative for that.

Now the six-day vacation at Camp Okawehna could begin.

Camp Okawehna was a summer camp located at Cedar Crest Campground in Lyles, Tennessee (within 50 miles of Nashville) for children with kidney disease; including transplant and dialysis patients.

Before dialysis, I'd never heard of this camp before, but I was so glad it existed.

During that time of my life I was very self-conscious of my body. The scars and tubes from/for treatment always kept me with a shirt on *and* in the house. But finally, I'd come across a Camp that catered to us dialysis patients and recipients.

I remember the day as if it was yesterday.

All of us from LeBonheur dialysis unit gathered on the bus early that morning, both patients and nurses. We all met up at some local park where everyone who was going to Camp O from Memphis joined us. Traveling to Camp O was fun.

Antonio "Tony", his brother Jermaine, Kenotta "Ken" and my cousin, Jerika, and I were all joking and laughing the whole ride, in the back of the bus.

When we made it to Camp Okawehna I noticed a lot of land and fields. I quickly realized that it'll be a lot of outdoor play. I was excited about that.

"Welcome to Camp Okawehna, guys," I heard over the intercom as the bus slowly came to a stop. As we pulled up, I noticed a group of people waiting for us, standing outside the bus.

The people who were waiting greeted us with smiling faces, a garland and Camp Okawehna gear. They provided us with draw string backpacks, shirts, water bottles, etc.

Shortly after receiving our luggage, they separated us into groups of six; four patients/recipients and two counselors. They separated the boys and girls and assigned a cabin name; my group was called Dogwood II.

Once everything was established and all the team members arrived and was checked off, we then separated and went to our cabins.

The cabins were really cool. They were built in the woods. For those who knew me, knew that I didn't do woods! That equaled bugs, especially with being in the south during Summer, mosquitos were sure to be on the hunt by nightfall.

Also, there wasn't any air-conditioned units, but it was a pretty good breeze due to most of the sunlight being blocked by towering trees, so it wasn't too bad.

I learned really quickly that I was on a real outdoors camping experience. I was a little nervous, but I was excited to experience...

As we all got settled in, we got to know each other a bit and joked around. Giving each other silly names. My name was Chicken Legs (I have little legs). I remembered the two counselors christened nicknames. Bob's name was Turkey Neck and Ryan's name was Curly.

The other campers' names were Fatback, Subway and Chicken Wing.

We had a lot of fun together.

I just knew this was exactly what I needed to disconnect from my reality back home.

I believed they gave us an hour to separate into groups before the entire Camp met up and ate dinner in a huge luncheon area that mimicked a Cafeteria in Grade School.

Camp O had a variety of things for us to do that kept us active and enjoying ourselves for the week.

One of the first events that took place was the Pinewood Derby. We got to sand down, paint and add wheels to pre-made cars. The next day was a big competition for the entire Camp and we raced each other.

We had many arts and crafts activities (which I personally loved).

We had scavenger hunts, trips to a local pool, outdoor bouncers, slides, basketball games, talent shows and even a prom.

Camp was definitely an experience I'd never forget for as long as I lived. I always said that one day I was going to come back and be a counselor. This experience completely changed my outlook on life and how I looked at myself.

I would love to give back to the next generation of transplant patients and make new memories.

Leaving camp that morning was hard; just like any other trip when it's time to go home. I'd made many friends, took plenty of pictures and left with many memories encapsulated in my heart. I promised that I would return to Camp O one day and share my funny stories about what Camp O was like when I was there.

As everyone filed onto the bus, I couldn't help but think of how grateful and blessed I was to get to experience Camp O for a whole week.

I'd never been to a Camp that was specifically for kidney disease patients and recipients…

It was something I'd never forget. It was nice to check out from reality and my issues and have fun, be a teenager and enjoy myself for the first time in a long time.

This week of stress therapy was much needed.

Now I was refreshed…

Ready to tackle whatever was headed my way.

CHAPTER 9:

FINALLY, I BELIEVE

As we're heading home from camp, I was cold on the bus. I found myself bundled up in my jacket. Getting lost in my head…reminiscing about my life-changing experience at Camp O and my favorite parts that took place. Out of all the memories, I thought of how confident I was now after camp, it really changed my perspective on how I saw and lived my life and how I viewed myself as a hemodialysis patient. I give all the credit to this girl named Erica, from the swimming pool.

Having a talk with her literally changed my mindset, self-confidence and how I viewed myself after hearing her story.

As my friends and other patients engaged one another, my mind drifted in retrospect.

I was remembering when I met Erica …

A COUPLE DAYS AGO…

I BELIEVED IT WAS A beautiful Wednesday afternoon at Camp Okawehna. The day some of us went to the swimming pool. During this time in my life I was very self-conscious of my body and how people would look at me.

Those of us who were going swimming had to have the proper dressing on our dialysis catheter, covered and secured. Before each of us went to the pool, if we haven't got the dressing put on after treatment we stopped by the dialysis unit that was at the camp to get the catheters wrapped properly, myself and the group, who cabined with me, went back to our cabin to get changed for the pool.

I just knew I was going to have a shirt on with my swimming trunks.

Once we all were ready, we headed out the cabin. It was then Tony noticed that I wasn't going shirtless like him, Jermaine and Ken.

"You're going with a shirt on?" he asked.

"Uhh, yeah!" I enthused.

Tony held the door open for all of us to come out of cabin.

"But, why? We aren't going with no shirts," he instructed...

"Because I want to! I can't be showing off the goods to *everybody*," I said jokingly. To get him off my case about a freaking shirt.

The rest of the crew were shaking their heads, just tickled with laughter.

"Chicken legs…you are one silly guy," said Curly.

Did Curly just call me 'Chicken Legs'?

"I mean…I'm just saying," I went on. "He asked about my shirt. I answered. Y'all wasn't expecting that one, huh?" I laughed.

"No," Tony said.

"Well stop asking me silly questions and I won't have to answer them; ain't no telling what I might say, what comes up…comes out!"

I was joking around.

After a few moments, we walked towards the van. For the ride to the pool.

"Yeah we see that!" Turkey Neck said, laughing.

We talked amongst each other until everyone who was going to the pool was loaded on the van. It was packed, too. I had loads of fun! The ride itself, with all of us being excited to go to the pool, was memorable. I couldn't wait to cool off in the pool during this hot day.

Once we arrived at the pool, my entire jaw hit the concrete. Now I knew there were many types of dialysis patients attending Camp O…but seeing everyone in regular clothes…they didn't really look like patients. Just regular kids…

But *now* that they were shirtless and in swimming suits, I saw many different patients. I saw patients and recipients, lung and heart recipients. I was so shocked and amazed at how open and free those campers were. I couldn't believe my eyes.

I saw many of their scars. Developed from the aftermath of transplant surgeries. I took in the bandage dressings over their dialysis lines, so the lines remained dry and intact.

The group split up once we got to the pool. I was planted at the entrance gate for a couple seconds. Taking it all in. Like…those folks just got their scars and bandages showing like they didn't have a single care in the world.

As I continued to observe the pool and the environment, I noticed a teenager named Erica. She was a sixteen-year-old, two-year post kidney transplant recipient.

We talked a couple times.

I went and sat next to her on the bank and put my feet in the water.

"Hey, Erica." I said. I was approaching her.

"Hey, Boo! How's it going?" she asked and looked up at me.

"Hot, Girl! It is *too* hot out here," I said as I put my towel down to sit on before putting feet in the water.

Well...if you take off that shirt you might catch a lil breeze here and there," she suggested.

"Nah! I don't take my shit off. I don't know these folks like that," I said.

"Know them like what? We're at a pool! Ain't nobody here gonna laugh at you. You ain't the only skinny one out here. *Plus,* we all had to go through the dialysis phase at some point on our respective journeys before some of us got our transplants.

"You see me," she went on. "I'll show my scar in a minute. It ain't no shame in mine. Embrace it! We all have scars and imperfections! We may not like certain things about our bodies; but we're all here to support one another. We're all going through this dialysis thing and transplants *together.*

"We are not going to look at you any different than you already are. With your silly, *chocolate* self..." she explained with a touch of humor.

"I see. They're just all out with it. It messed me up when I initially saw this...Did you see me standing by the gate?" I asked.

"Yeah! I saw you! Up there looking like a deer in headlights." She laughed.

"Girl! I was taken aback. The whole idea of dialysis patients being outside with their shirts off seems otherworldly, in a sense. In broad day light? I wouldn't have *never* done or seen any of this back home," I explained.

"Right. See...things back home, for you, is different. You don't relate anyone... but here at Camp Okawehna...*we* support and have fun together," she explained.

"Yeah I see. I'm really starting to like it here. I'm glad I came, it's taken all that stress I was dealing with back home off my shoulders, allowing me to finally relax and enjoy myself with people who are just like me," I admitted.

"*Exactly*! So, enjoy yourself!" she shouted and caught me off guard by pulling my shirt up and around my head, taking it completely off.

"Ooop!" I blurted in shock, wrapping my arms around my chest.

"Oh, come on! Its off now! *You did it!* Just enjoy yourself and be free," she said. She smiled and twirled my shirt over her head like a helicopter.

Before too long I laughed and unraveled my arms; exposing my upper body to the great outdoors for the first time, ever, since I started dialysis treatments. I reluctantly embraced having my shirt off in public and I must say, it was so refreshing to feel the breeze on my skin.

It was scary for the first few seconds, but once it dawned on me that no one was staring at me like the swamp thing, I became more relaxed. They paid me no mind!

I became more relaxed and comfortable. Before we left the pool, I was in the water with the others. Having a good time being free from judgement, insecurities, self-hate, doubt and low self-esteem, I embraced my uniqueness. With the other patients and recipients.

Now I knew what it felt like to be free and accept yourself for who and what you were.

Now I believed!

I FINALLY BELIEVE!

I had cracked the code to this whole dialysis thang. After all the days, hours, minutes, months and a year on dialysis…it took *one week at Camp O!* to realize that it was not about being on dialysis…

It was about the way I looked…

The scars on my body told a story…

My story!

It was about how I felt; it was about accepting me, *completely*. Just the way I was. Having a good support system kept me focused…

Knowing people who related to me and my ordeal helped me remain strong, assertive and humble. I embraced my journey.

There was one thing I took from Erica and from my delightful time at Camp O in a whole. You were not gonna feel your best every day, but at least you were blessed to live another day. So, enjoy life! Make the best of it.

Frankly, I should stop being so hard on myself because I had kidney disease. Everything happened for a reason.

It was up to me to figure that out along the way.

Until then, I was gonna enjoy every day as if it was my last. I was gonna live with no regrets. I was gonna take risks, have fun and help others as much as I could…*when* I could.

As I continued to lounge in my seat on the bus, I was reminiscing over my week-long stress therapy at Camp O.

I was feeling good. I was ready to get back home and continue to tackle my journey with a more enlightened and positive mindset.

Nothing could stop me or hold me back now. I was ready to take on the challenges that came my way…

And I couldn't wait to see what happens next…

Part 3:

Through the Storm Comes Open Doors

CHAPTER 10:

THIS IS THE DAY THE LORD HAS MADE

Well the time had come! Transplant Day! The day every dialysis patient dreamt of. It was Tuesday, July 15, 2005. Approximately 3:00 in the morning. I was just like a restless kid on Christmas Eve who couldn't sleep due to the excitement for presents.

However, this new present wouldn't be no new clothes or electronic device.

This was the gift of life.

Being one of the few patients to get a second chance at life, I was deeply humbled. I couldn't be anything but thankful and highly favored for the blessing of receiving one of my dads' kidneys.

I would never be able to repay him for this, as I laid in my hospital bed, I was watching the clock tick away. My arm with the IV was elevated. I couldn't help but think of how excited I was just to make it to this day.

The waiting was finally over. No more dialysis treatments, crazy diets and uncontrollable mood swings. I envisioned how everything was going to play out.

The thought of the upcoming surgery, post-surgery and how I would feel after it was over.

What would be my first meal? I'd have more free time to finish high school. I could hang out with my friends and finally be cured from kidney disease.

Excitedly, I continued to think of the many events and goals I was setting after my transplant.

I finally drift off.

A couple hours passed, and my doctor interrupted my nap by lightly knocking on the door.

"Artavius... Good Morning" The doctor said as she and about two other doctors came into the room. They assembled at the foot of my bed.

"Good Morning," I said softly. I wiped my eyes and sat up, trying to wake up.

"Oh, we didn't mean to wake you up–but today is the day! Transplant day! You Ready?" she asked.

"Yes, I am!" I answered, filled with joy.

"Okay, great! How you are feeling this morning, outside of the excitement?" she asked.

"I'm doing great. I couldn't really sleep last night due to the anticipation and from my arm hurting with this IV. My nurse suggested that I prop my arm up.

"Once I did it finally stopped hurting," I explained.

"Great. We'll be sure to let the nurse know if you have any more pain before the surgery today. Alright, so right now we just got the word that your dad is now across the street at The Med hospital and is being prepped for surgery. It's about 8:15 now, so I say about 10 o'clock we should be hearing something back, okay?

"So just stay put," she went on. "You know you can't eat or drink before surgery. We don't want to have to reschedule the surgery. It shouldn't be much longer after they've removed your father's kidney before we come for you to perform the procedure," she announced.

"Okay, cool. Thank you," I responded.

"Alright, we'll see you soon" she said as she and the other doctors waved and smiled. They headed towards the door.

"Okay," I responded. I also waved.

Once they left, I sat up in the bed and gazed out the window and went into a prayer…

Dear Lord,

I come to you early this morning, Father, just to say thank you. Thank you for waking me up this morning; thank you for allowing me to see another day, especially this day, Father. It's been a long eighteen months with dialysis, but I thank You. Some patients have been waiting longer and I can't complain. I ask that You be with my father as he undergoes his portion of the surgery. Please let everything go well with no complications, Lord. You've brought us this far for this moment and I believe that You didn't bring us this far just to bring us this far. I know you have a purpose for the both of us and Lord if it is Your Will, let it be done. In your name I pray, Amen...

Two Hours Later...

"Alright, Mr. Veasey. Are you ready?" my nurse asked as she came in my room.

"Yes, Ma'am," I turned and said. I was already up on the side of the bed, looking out the window.

"Well, let's go," she said. She helped me to the other bed she had pushed just outside my room.

"How's my dad doing?" I asked.

"He's great! We've got the call that they successfully removed the kidney and it should be heading here shortly," she stated as she walked to the side of the bed to get my IV and fluids monitor.

"Oh, thank God. Glad he's okay," I said out loud as I climbed in the other bed, ready to go.

"I'll be here when you get back," Momma said. She was sitting on the couch, on the phone as usual.

"Okay..."

"Alright, next stop--*transplant*!" the nurse said as she walked out the room, with my IV fluids and monitor.

On my way down to surgery all I could remember was feeling this warm, tingling sensation all over my body. I knew it was me being nervous and excited at the same time.

"Are you excited?" the nurse asked.

We waited for the elevator to come up.

"Yes, very! I'm a little nervous also," I replied.

"Oh, you'll be just fine. No need to be nervous at all" she said.

"Yeah, I know. The lord got me; as my Grandma use to always tell me, 'The Lord didn't bring you this far just to bring me this far'. In other words, He didn't bring me this far to leave me now," I explained.

"Amen" she agreed.

The rest of the ride to surgery was quiet. I was content with everything in my life that happened up to this point. As we were going down the hall, I was having flashbacks of everything I went through from birth; family functions, getting the call when I had to go on dialysis, the first day of dialysis, crazy nights in the hospital, mood swings, depression, suicidal thoughts, loneliness, Camp O and fun times in the dialysis unit here at LeBonheur.

Now at this point I was a few minutes away from my transplant and out of nowhere a piece of my purpose in life hit me like a Spartan kick to the face; I was put here to share this journey and how I made it through.

This was what my grandma was talking about when she said all of this would make sense in due time. God did everything for a reason. Now it made sense. Now I understood why He took me through all the challenges.

He wanted me to use my testimony, my trials and tribulations to be an inspiration to others who were on their journey to transplantation.

I get it!

That was it!

This was how I intended to keep the promise I made with God, about if He got me through this. I would do everything in my power to help somebody else. From there it was like instant gratification and *appreciation* for the Lord. He trusted me enough to take me through what He did. He kept me strong **ENOUGH** to hold on; He kept me strong **ENOUGH** to not give up; and He kept me wise **ENOUGH** to be able to see it through.

I couldn't believe it, but I figured out my assignment and a piece of my purpose in life.

I was here to be a living testimony.

I thanked Him for what He did. I was blessed because I'd learned that He would never put more on us than we could bare. At the time of the storm it might feel like the weight of the world was literally sitting on our shoulders as if we were being punished by God. Little did I know that God gave His hardest task to His strongest children and I was blessed to say that I was one of the chosen ones.

"Well, here we are," Denese announced as we pulled up to the closed doors of the surgery room.

After a few beats, the double doors opened.

"Good morning!" Denese said to the doctors that were revealed as the double doors opened.

"Hi, Denese. How are you?" one of the nurses said.

"I'm good," Denese responded, transporting me on the bed.

"Hello, Artavius. Today's the big day. Are you ready?" one of the doctors asked.

"Yes, ma'am," I answered with a smile on my face. "I've waited a year and half for this day, so yes I'm ready!"

"Alright…we're *now* waiting on Dr. Santiago so we can get the procedure started. We've gotten word that your dad is doing great. They removed the kidney successfully and he's now in recovery," the doctor informed.

"Okay, great," I responded.

The double doors opened again.

"Good morning, everybody!" Dr. Santiago greeted everyone as he walked into the surgery department.

"Good morning!" everybody said.

Dr. Santiago placed his hand on my shoulder and asked me, "So, are you ready, Big Guy?"

"Yes, Sir," I enthused. I looked up at him, smiling.

"Okay…" Dr. Santiago instructed the other doctors. "Let's take Artavius to the operating table and set up. The kidney is headed here now, and we want to be ready for the kidney when it arrives."

"Yes, Sir." The doctors responded.

"Give me a few and I'll meet y'all in the operating room to perform the transplant," Dr. Santiago said, and he headed over to the sink to wash his hands.

"Alright, Artavius. Well, good luck with the surgery," Denese said. "If I don't see you when you get back upstairs you take care of yourself and that new kidney."

She hugged me and left the surgery room.

"Alright, thank you and I will," I said.

I smiled and waved as the double doors were closing behind her.

"Alright, Artavius...let's get you set up," the surgical tech insisted.

The doctors then rolled me around the corner to the operating area and the surgical tech begun to go over what she was doing.

She hooked up me up to an IV and asked me the flavor of choice for my sleep gas. I chose my favorite, strawberry.

After choosing the flavor, I thought to myself...

Well, this is my last time on this table. After this I will have my life back. I can finish school normally and go back to school with my friends. No more home school, crazy diets and feeling weak; above all, *bye Felisha!* to all the mood swings...

"Alright. We're gonna get started now, okay?" the tech mentioned.

I nodded in agreement. I remembered from my last surgery, the sleeping gas and the tech talking to me, it was like I was being hypnotized...she kept repeating herself over and over and over again; this time, I just nodded.

"Okay, inhale deep breaths for me and let's count backwards from one hundred," the tech suggested.

I nodded again. I knew from the last surgery it wouldn't take ten seconds before I was knocked out, so I nodded as she counted every number down from one hundred and I went into prayer.

"Dear Lord...

"Here we go! I leave it all in Your hands now. I want to thank You in advance for getting me to this point in my journey. You've gotten me this far and I know you're not gonna--"

I prayed before the anesthesia kicked in. During the time of my surgery I was in a deep sleep and fell in a bad dream. What was only a couple of hours felt like forever in the dream when I finally raised up fast in a deep gasp, breathing, clad in a light sweat.

"Artavius, calm down, calm down!" The nurse shouted as he tried to lower me down on the bed.

I was still in a panic. I wildly looked around, breathed hard. I did not recognize where I was. After a few seconds of the nurse trying to calm me down and help me realize it was just a bad dream I calmed down realizing I was back in ICU recovering. The nurse then released from trying to hold me down and I look at the clock at saw it was 4:52pm.

"Geez, Artavius! You just had a kidney transplant. You must relax. No jumping up just yet. You're gonna pop all your staples out," he explained.

"I was being chased," I said, exasperated. I held my arm over my forehead, *trying* to catch my breath.

"Oh, it was just a bad dream; being under anesthesia will sometimes produce bad dreams," he summarized.

"Yeah! I see that now," I implored, as my breathing returned to its normal pace.

"Who was chasing you?" he asked.

"Some Giant Cheerios" I said, lying there with my eyes closed.

"*Cheerios?* You must have eaten some?" he asked, laughing.

"Uh, sir…you are laughing a lil too hard. And no, I didn't eat any. I don't even *like* Cheerios. They taste all plain and need some sugar added for my liking.

"Those thangs were so big and going so fast!" I parlayed. "I was running like an Olympic medalist in a 400-meter dash being chasing by flesh eating pit bulls. Now, I always dreamed of running track, but, man! I was running for my life. Literally," I described.

"Well, *hey*…maybe you should sign up to run in a race or marathon," he suggested.

"If it's anything like that dream, I don't think I want to do that no more," I said.

"No, it's nothing like that! I think you'll like it," he said.

"I don't know. I'll think about it," I said.

"Okay, well try to relax," he urged, "and we'll notify your family and doctors that you've awaken from your surgery."

He then walked out and closed the separation curtain behind him.

I laid there on my back, looking around. I didn't see or hear any other patients or children.

"Thank you, Lord," I said to myself after taking a deep breath and softly closing my eyes to relax.

Before I drifted back to sleep. my surgeon, Dr. Santiago, came into my sectioned area.

"*Hey big guy!* How you are feeling?" Dr. Santiago asked. He stepped closer to my bed.

"I'm alright…a little sore," I said softly.

"Good. That's normal after surgery. Well, I wanted to let you know that everything went great. I talked to the nurses here in recovery and everything seems to be good. We're gonna take you back up to your room. We'll keep you overnight just to make sure everything is okay before we release you okay?" he said.

"Okay" I responded.

"Now take it easy because you have staples along your right-side, across from your navel. You don't want to make many sudden movements; keep it to a minimal. At least until you're healed, and we take the staples out.

"We'll see you, in about a week, back at the transplant clinic so we could check out the kidney. If all is well, then we'll see you in about two months; to have your staples removed," he said.

"Okay, thank you," I responded.

"No problem." he said and reached for a handshake.

"Thank you," I said sincerely as I shook his hand.

"You're so welcome. Take care of yourself kid," he insisted.

"I promise you, I will if that's the last thing I do," I vowed.

"Alright, well, I'll come see you in the morning to update you on everything before we discharge you," he said.

He was backing out of the area I was in.

"Okay," I replied.

A few minutes passed by before the nurse came back in and started wheeling me back to my room on the sixth floor. As we were rolling, it remained a quiet ride. I was in my head trying to process everything that'd happened; from the surgery, the dream and my journey up to this point, it all just felt so surreal.

Once we got back to my room, Momma was sitting in the chair closest to the window, talking on her earpiece.

Momma and the nurse helped me transition from the wheeled bed to my room bed.

"There you go. Do you need anything else at the moment before I leave, Artavius?" the nurse asked.

"No, ma'am. Thank you," I said softly. I slowly adjusted my body. I tried to get in a comfortable position so I wouldn't hurt so much.

"Alright, well if anything comes up or if you need anything, just hit the red nurse button on your remote, okay?" she announced as she backed out of the room.

"Okay, thank you," I said. I tried to relax.

As the nurse walked out, I was still try'na find a comfortable position.

Momma come over to my bedside.

"What's wrong?" she asked.

"Try'na get comfortable to keep from hurting," I said as I continued to adjust my body.

"You want me to tell the nurse to bring you something for pain?" she suggested.

"Yes, please," I said.

She then grabbed the TV remote and called the front desk, asking them to bring me something for pain. I overheard the nurse say that my doctor ordered me some morphine for pain, and it should be there shortly.

"So, what's hurting?" Momma asked.

"My side. I guess that's where the new kidney's at," I responded.

"Have you looked at it?" she asked.

"Nah," I answered.

"Why not? Well, I want to see," she said. She begun to pull the cover off me and open my gown to see my scar.

"Ugh, Ma! I just got good and comfortable...plus you got to have consent to take off folk's clothes like that; that's called indecent exposure, ma'am.

"I'm gonna push that red button on you and tell those folks at the front desk that you're try'na take advantage of me," I joked with her.

She was struggling to untie my hospital gown.

"Boy hush. Ain't nobody try'na do nothing to you. With yo' crazy self," she said and laughed, untying the gown.

Once she got the gown open, there it was. The scar that saved and blessed me with a second chance at life. It looked to be about six to eight inches long. It was about an inch above my hip bone and stretched diagonally across and under my belly button.

"Dang look at all those staples," she said. She examined the scar.

"I know, right! It goes from my side all the way down close to my private part. Now are these regular staples like we use to staple paper and stuff?" I asked.

"Nal, boy! Those are surgical staples," she answered.

"Aw, okay. I was about to say! That's why I'm hurting. They use those cheap ole' staples, look like a good one hundred of them," I joked.

"You're so silly. There are probably about thirty or forty," she guessed.

"I don't know. All I know is that there are a whole bunch of those thangs," I said.

"Okay. You have staples on your scar so be careful, Tay, because you can bust it and pop the staples out. Then your wound could get infected. You can't be doing too much moving, especially bending down," she explained.

"Yeah, the doctor said that and to take it easy," I told her.

"I know you don't want it to get infected and you have to go through this again, right?" she asked.

"I sholl don't! I've come too far to go back now," I said.

"Alright then, so be careful" she said.

"I will."

"Yo' Grandma called to see how you were doing, but you were in recovery. I told her I'll have you call her when you get back up here," she said.

"Okay, I'll call her," I said.

"Here's your phone," she said, handing me my phone.

I called Gma Shirley. She was sitting with my daddy in his hospital room while Momma stayed with me. I inquired about my father...

"Yeah, he alright," said Gma Shirley through the receiver. "He's sitting up here, high off his pain meds. He said he was in a little pain, but he seems to be good now. He's been talking and asking about you...to see how everything went and were you okay...

"Here he goes. Spanky (my dad's nickname), Tay's on the phone," she said, handing him the phone.

"Hello," he said softly.

"Hello," I responded.

"What's up, man. How are you feeling?" he asked.

"I'm ok, a little sore, but I'm good. How are you feeling?" I asked.

"I was hurting a little a few minutes ago but they brought me some pain medicine so I'm alright now" he confided.

"Yeah...I'm waiting on them to bring mine now," I said.

"Aw, okay," he said.

"Well, we did it!" I announced.

"Yep we did, son!" he agreed.

"I'mma have to show you, when we get together, the kidney bulging on my side" I suggested.

Ha, Ha! "You got that grown man kidney in you boy," he joked.

"Whatever." I snickered.

"Now you better take care of it; if they tell me you're not, I'mma come get it back," he joked.

"Really? You just gonna come get it back like that?" I asked, joking with him.

"Yeah, if you ain't doing right" he said.

"Okay, daddy...I think those pain meds are getting to you now. So I'mma let you go and hit you up later when they release me from here," I said.

"When they say they was gonna discharge you?" he asked. "My doctor said if everything good I should be leaving tomorrow."

"Aw, okay...They said I'll be getting discharged tomorrow, too, *supposedly*," I answered.

"Yeah, okay." he said.

"Alright, well I love you and I'll talk to you later, okay," I concluded.

"Okay and love you too, son," he said.

"Alright, bye bye," I said.

"Alright..."

I hung up.

Soon as I got off the phone with my daddy and grandma, the nurse came in with this machine that looked like a personal sized pump.

"Hello, Artavius! Here's your pain meds," the nurse said as she rolled the little machine over to connect to my IV.

"Oh, okay. It looks like my own personal size pump; it comes with a trigger push button too" I said jokingly.

She tittered happily. "Yes sir. How this works is whenever you're having pain just push the button. Within a few minutes you should be feeling better," she summarized.

"Oh, okay—cool. Um, can I push the button now to stop the little pain I have?" I asked.

"Yes, of course! Whenever you're experiencing pain just push the button," she further explained.

"Okay, so is it a certain amount of times I can push it?" I asked, curious.

"No, however many you like," she informed.

"Oooh, okay. Thank you," I said with a smile.

"Oh, Lord! *Now* he about to be up here high off the morphine. You shouldn't have told him that, ma'am," Momma said and shook her head.

"Oh, he's fine. As long as he's not in any pain, he's good," the nurse said.

"No, I'm not, Ma! She said when I feel pain press the button so I'mma follow the directions my nurse gave me, and only press the button when I'm in pain," retorted. I rebuked Momma's assumption.

"Yeah, press the button ONE time," Mama said. "Not two, three and four times."

"I know, I know," I said.

"Un-huh, we'll see." Momma continued to shake her head.

My nurse was amused. "You two are silly, is there anything else you need?" the nurse asked.

"No, ma'am, thank you so much" I replied.

"Oh, no problem. Your dinner should be here in a few. I know you're starving," the nurse mentioned.

"Yes, I am," I agreed.

"Alright, well y'all have a great rest of your evening. If you need anything, just push the button and let us know," she said while she backed out of the room.

"Oh, we will! *Thanks*!" I said and I laughed.

After the nurse left the room, Momma and I joked around a little more. Over the next hour or so my dinner came. I ate it and before I knew it, I was knocked out!

Sleep…

Every time I felt a sting or pressure of pain, I pressed that button for morphine.

It was so good.

I slept through the night without any pain or disturbance from the nurses coming in and out to take my blood pressure and temperature.

As far as I knew…

Chapter 11:

My Second Chance at Life

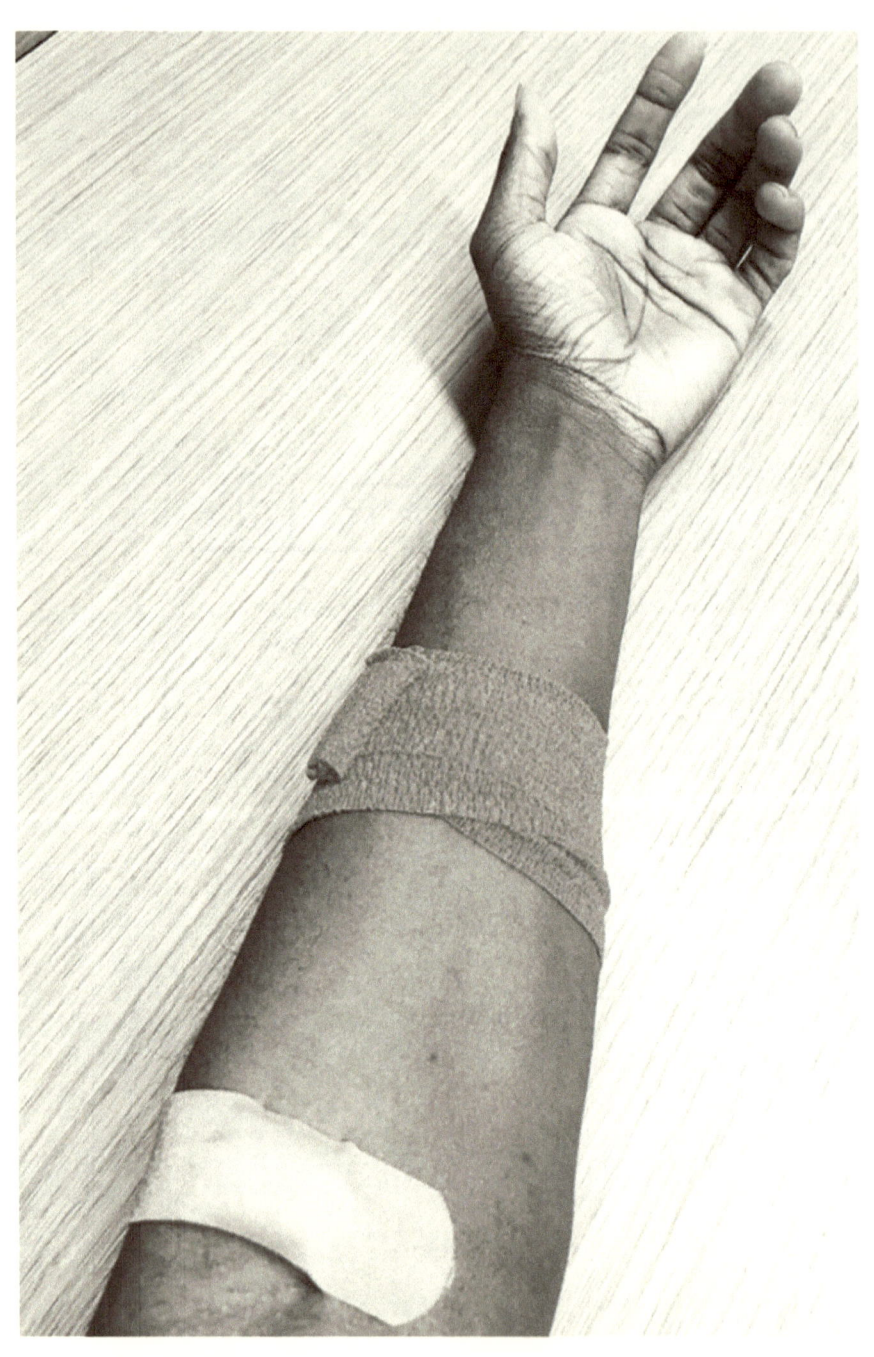

130 BECOMING A LIVING TESTIMONY

The next day, July 16, 2005, I awaked to the knocks-on-the-door from morning shift nurses and doctors. I was fully covered with my blanket pulled over my head. I was all comfortable and relaxed from the morphine.

Someone knocked on my door.

"Good morning, Artavius." The doctors greeted me as they entered the room.

"Morning," I said softly.

"How are you feeling?" the male doctor asked.

"I'm okay," I answered.

"How did you sleep last night?" he continued.

"Oh, he slept really good. They had to bring him another machine of morphine," Momma interrupted.

"Oh, really," he said.

"Well, see…what had happened was ---"

"He was tearing that button up, sitting up here high off them pain meds," Momma interrupted me.

Hahahaha! "That's okay. As long as he's feeling good and not hurting, he's fine," the female doctor responded.

"See, Ma! Always try'na snitch on somebody. You know what they say: snitches get stitches. My nurse said if I have ANY pain press the button. It didn't matter how many times. All they care about is me not hurting.

"As long as I'm feeling good, ha! Why you try'na snitch on me? Because, baby, *I feel gooddd!*" I said, breaking into Stephanie Mills' "I Feel Good" song.

"Oh, you have a nice voice, Artavius. I didn't know you could sing." the female doctor complimented.

"No, no, no, no...I can't sing. I can hold a note, there's a difference" I joked.

"You are so silly. Well, we can see you're definitely feeling great this morning," the female doctor continued.

"Yes, ma'am," I responded excitingly.

"Have you had a chance to get up and walk yet?" Dr. Santiago asked.

"No, sir. Since I came back from recovery, I've been in the bed. I was hurting so bad I didn't really want to move much, but since I've been on the morphine, I been good," I explained.

"Okay, good, but before we discharge you, we need you to walk and get use to that new kidney. You will be a little sore, but the more you walk, the easier it'll be. Be careful and make sure you're with someone. You don't want to trip or fall and mess anything up," Dr. Santiago continued.

"You ain't said nothing but the word," I said. I propped up quickly in my hospital bed.

"Hold up Tay. Be careful, now. You're gonna bust one of those staples. Take your time," Momma reminded me.

"Yes, take it easy. You're not 100% just yet. Your scar has to heal first," Dr. Santiago said.

"Okay, okay. I'm sorry. I got a little excited," I apologized.

"Well you guys go ahead. And like I said...we'll check in with you later, Artavius, okay?" Dr. Santiago said as he and the other two doctors waved bye and walked out the door.

After the doctors left, Momma lectured me about walking and being careful with the safety of the kidney. Time went on as we talked. I ate real breakfast without worrying about the sodium, potassium and fluid intake. I could finally just eat and drink how much I wanted. I was very happy about that.

My first-time walking since the surgery consisted of a slight stroll around my hospital bed into the bathroom to use it.

Once I finished doing what I was doing, I went up to the sink to wash my hands. I took a good look at myself and noticed how clear my skin has gotten.

"Dang, my face is all clear; that ugly, stubborn bump on my nose is finally gone. Now I'm clean, clear and under control, baby! Look like I got a few shades brighter, too!

"They better watch out! I'mma be team red bone in a minute," I said, hyping myself up while I looked myself over in the mirror.

"Boy, stop, with yo' crazy self," Momma said. She laughed and watched me act silly in the mirror.

"Don't be hating 'cause you ain't this fine. I just got my braces off, too! Teeth all straight and pearly white! *Oooohhweeeee!* I need to schedule a photoshoot! I'm just looking *too* good to keep all this to myself. *I got to* **SHARE IT WITH THE WORLD!**

"...The ugly duckling phase is gone; sexy Tay is here now! **THE WORLD BETTER WATCH OUT!**" I continued joking in the mirror.

"Boy come on so you can walk with your crazy self," Momma shouted as I finished washing my hands and came out of the bathroom.

Initially, I started off walking around the room, then Momma walked up and down the halls with me while I joked with the nurses at the front desk, until I got tired.

Long story short, the doctors came back and insisted that I stay another day or two to be sure everything is good before they discharge me.

She told me that my labs and results came back good. My creatinine was a 0.7, which was basically a perfect match, but they wanted to take a few more blood samples for another test.

I was a little upset because I was looking forward to going home and sleeping in my own bed, but I made a deal with my doctor, that if they'll bring me some French vanilla ice cream and some chocolate chip cookies from Subway I'll stay.

She had the staff bring me small cups of blue bell ice cream, but they didn't have any cookies. I was fine with that, so I ate my ice cream.

Surprisingly, Gma Shirley and **TT** Wanda came to see me and brought me some snacks.

The following days went well. Friends and family members dropped by to say hey and hung out while I ate my ice cream and snacked on whatever I could get my hands on.

We had pizza and played games, enjoying each other's company while supporting my big moment…getting a kidney transplant.

I slept really well, thanks again to the morphine pump. I was later discharged from the hospital about one o'clock that afternoon on July 19th, 2005.

The ride in a wheelchair from my hospital room out to the car was such a rewarding and liberating experience.

I finally felt like I had my life back. Things were looking up for me.

The past four days in the hospital was the most fun I'd ever had in a long time while in the hospital.

I knew it was a lot I still had to learn and experience now that I was a kidney transplant recipient, but I just wanted to enjoy the moment and be grateful…

For my second chance at life.

CHAPTER 12:

ONE STEP FORWARD, TWO STEPS BACK

136 BECOMING A LIVING TESTIMONY

Well, here I was, once again! Back in the hospital. It was on the 29th Friday of the year 2006, July 21st... I was 16 years old. It'd been exactly one year and six days since my transplant. Things had been good. No complications or infections. The staples had been taken out and I'd healed up pretty good. I was on my last few days of my summer vacation before my 11th grade year and I'm super excited.

I just couldn't believe that in two more years I'd be graduating from high school! I attended Camp Okawehna again this past June and of course I had a blast. Now that I'd been transplanted, I was able to do more this year and not be exhausted like the first year.

This year my cousin, Jerika, and I was prom King and Queen and my group won second place in the talent show. It was a lot of fun and plenty more memories to go down in the books.

So now, I was sitting in my hospital room, intravenously receiving fluids because, apparently, I was dehydrated. I thought I drunk enough water, but clearly, I didn't.

There was an upside to all of this; it was just a one-day thing. I was supposed to get discharged after I get four bags of fluids. Fortunately, I wasn't too bombed out by being here because it was just dehydration. It wasn't for something too crazy, like a rejection or infection, so I was okay with this compared to the other two options.

This was the first time, after many previous stays in the hospital, that I actually got to rest and relax.

Yes, I know it was almost impossible to sleep or relax while in the hospital. The nurses came in and out, like, every ten to fifteen minutes to check your blood pressure and temperature…

This time I didn't mind because I knew I was okay, and I would be leaving the next day.

When the next day came, it was a little afternoon-ish when I was discharged. Now I was waiting for my nurse to come in and take the IV out of my arm.

While I waited, I got a visit from a familiar doctor, from when I was on dialysis. She informed me and my mom that Jessica, one of my good friends, while on dialysis, had passed a few months before.

Jessica was so much fun and full of life and loved her some Tay-Tay. I loved her, too! After every treatment, my area was right next to hers. When I was about to leave after treatment, every time I passed by, after changing into my clothes, she'd holler, "Tay-Tay! Where you finna go?"

I would always tell her, "I'm about to go, Jessica. I'll see you next treatment, okay?"

She'd be like, "You finna go home?"

I would agree, and then she'd ask when was I coming back and I would tell her or she'd get sad and teary eyed and then I'd hug her and tell her that I'd be back and I'd bring her a Sprite from home.

She loved Sprite; that was just about the only drink we could drink as dialysis patients. Only clear liquids, no dark drinks.

I really enjoyed her and her spirit; she was a lot of fun while we passed the time in treatment.

Jessica had been getting dialysis treatments for more than ten plus years.

In spite of what we went through on treatment (whether it was experiencing cramps, mood swings and pain from a lot of fluids being taken off, or screaming at our nurses to bring more blankets because we were cold); no matter who you were, if you walked passed Jessica's curtain you were going to speak to her and she'd make sure you do.

As we left the hospital, I was getting dropped off over Gma Shirley's house. In a daze, I was looking out of the window. I thought of the fun times I had when I was on dialysis…with the other patients who came into the Dialysis Unit on the third floor of the LeBonheur Children's Hospital.

It made me very grateful for my experiences and memories, but, more importantly, I got a newsflash about the vow I made to God.

I knew then…that tomorrow wasn't promised, and my grandmother used to always tell me, "Baby, nobody knows the day nor the hour. Make the best of every moment and experience you have because life is short."

From that exact moment, I knew I had to make a difference and spread the word about transplantation and how organ donations were saving lives.

Since then, my life panned out before my eyes.

I was having little to no complications with the new kidney, my body adjusted to the medication I was on and I went from taking seven pills a day to four.

My doctor visits stretched from once every month to once every three months, and now once every six months.

I'd been doing well. The health of my kidney was good. I was educating myself more on how to keep it healthy. I was able to graduate from Germantown High; Class of 2008.

I continued my education and went to Southwest Tennessee Community College. I graduated with honors, 'cum laude', with an associate degree in graphic design and interactive multimedia in 2012.

Here we were!

Eight years later, 2014.

I was the age of 24 years old.

I was a junior, undergrad, at Memphis College of Art, pursuing my bachelor's degree.

Just when I thought things were on the up and up, suddenly, I got hit with an infection as a result of the cold weather…

It sent me back to the hospital…

I was a bit scared; I was not gonna lie. Everything was going so well for me. I was a few months shy of my eighth-year kidney transplant anniversary, a year away from receiving my second degree.

By this time, I was a little local celebrity. When I was in my last year at Southwest, I was a part of their advertising team and campaign. Being a part of this campaign, I was featured on Southwest billboards, buses, magazines and commercials around the city of Memphis.

I'd admit and say that I was getting a little big headed, but I worked hard to achieve all those dreams and goals early; and I wasn't even twenty-five years old yet. So yeah, I was very proud of myself.

When the infection hit, I had to go back in the hospital for another couple of days. I was injected with antibiotics to kill off the infection.

I remembered lying in bed the first night, in the dark. I talked to God, asking him why did He bring me back to the hospital after being on a winning streak for almost eight years.

After waiting and waiting, He spoke to me in my dream that night. He told me how proud He was of me; and how He's blessed me with abundance and accomplishments.

Yet, I still failed at fulfilling my promise to Him. He was right. I was going through a lot of different changes. I was really focused on my education, art, and trying to build a brand for myself.

I wasn't making time for the transplant community…

I began to feel bad and ashamed. I asked God to help me and show me the direction He wanted me to go in. I kid you not, before I left my hospital room at Methodist Hospital, right in front of the bed, on the wall, hung a flyer for an upcoming kidney support group that was taking place in one of the meeting rooms in the hospital.

At that moment, I knew it was God.

Loud and clear.

All I could say was, "Okay, Your Will shall be done, and I will not let you down this time."

I vow…

CHAPTER 13:

BEING A BLESSING

When being a blessing to someone, my grandmother made sure I understood one thing, never expect nothing in return. "When you're able, you should always strive to give back and bless those along your journey when you can. Key words 'when you can'," she once told me.

In the words of Iyanla Vanzant, "You want to make sure your cup is full. What's in the cup is mine and what comes out the cup is for y'all-- My cup runneth over." (Psalm 23:5).

When you did a service out of kindness of your heart, do it just for that: the kindness of your heart. You didn't do it to get something in return or use the act as a burden to the person.

You didn't constantly remind a person of what you'd done or how if it wasn't for you that person wouldn't have X-Y-Z; that was the opposite of being a blessing. That was called "condemnation."

Even though that'd been one of the hardest lessons for me to grasp, as time went by, I'd become more self-aware and I'd been taking care of myself first (keeping my cup full), before I go and try to help or be a blessing to someone else.

As I'd gotten older, I'd come to realize that my biggest blessing to the world was the gift of transparency. To be relatable, or to be a voice for those patients in the hospital and in dialysis units across the world. It was always a dream of mine and it was also my way of living up to the promise I'd made to God.

I remembered when the day came for the support group meeting. I was so excited. I knew I was on the right path to fulfilling my promise and I couldn't wait to see what He had in stored for me on this journey, of sharing my story with others.

Once I got to the room where the meeting was held, at Methodist University Hospital, I noticed a big, brown wooden table with chairs.

Later in the meeting, as other patients arrived, I'd realized that the group was full of dialysis patients and transplant recipients.

Suffice it to say, we had intimate table talk where we, the recipients, introduced ourselves. We disclosed the type of transplant we had, how long we'd been transplanted, and we individually shared our stories.

Out of this particular group, I was the youngest and had my kidney the longest. It was so rewarding and humbling to say the least. The respect and love that washed over me from the support group was just unbelievable.

After each recipient shared their stories, we had a question and answer session with the patients. There was an array of recipients at this meeting; we had two kidney recipients (including myself). And we had a liver, a heart and a lungs recipient as well.

I was more than honored to be amongst the diverse group of transplant recipients and to hear their journey to transplantation, and where they were now.

We shared tips and tricks on how to keep a healthy organ and what to look for when it came to signs of infection. The session was very informative.

We also talked about medication and our experiences the first year of being transplanted.

It was an amazing experience!

As I went to more of the support group meetings every month, the crowd and patients grew larger. To the point we eventually had to get a bigger table and room.

The reaction and response I got from both the patients and nurses was empowering. I was now ready to spread my wings and share my story online.

At this point in my life, I'd graduated from Memphis College of Arts with a bachelor's degree in graphic design. I had a bit of a following and supporters. I was best known for my comical sense of humor, personality and my creativity.

Very few of them knew that I was a kidney recipient.

I then began to share my story on each of my online platforms and mix my world of ART and Transplantation. I'd had great opportunities. I'd been blessed tremendously with artistic talent, yet I hadn't quite found my way or stride when it came to the transplant community.

For months, as I went to various support groups, I tried to find other avenues to reach out or to collaborate with likeminded individuals, but I wasn't really having much luck.

It was the fall of 2015. I was 25 years old. I'd made it to the big milestone of ten years post-transplant. I was now having a once a year check-up with my kidney doctor.

I remembered one time when I went to the clinic for a check-up. I was sitting in the waiting room, bored, without a signal on my phone. I just happened to see a group of magazines on the table.

As I was reaching to get a magazine, I saw a brochure of an organization called the Mid-South Transplant Foundation (MSTF). Apparently, they were putting together a team for the bi-yearly Transplant Games of America.

Completely caught off guard, I was instantly sold and aware that God had yet again pointed me in the direction He wanted me to go. Just like the time I saw the poster for the support group. All I could do was accept the task and reach out to the organization.

Meeting the Mid-South Transplant Foundation was like having an extension to my support group family and friends, all bunched up into one big, loving organization.

The Mid-South Transplant Foundation worked to connect people in need of life-saving organs or tissue transplants with donors.

They also served as an organ donor network for counties in West Tennessee, North Mississippi and East Arkansas. They worked diligently to establish close relationships with the hospitals and the communities they served. (www.midsouthtransplant.org).

This organization was exactly what I was looking for and I wanted to be a part of it. The atmosphere was welcoming and inspirational. I knew I was hooked and wanted to stick around for a little bit.

The Executive Director, Mrs. Kim Van Frank, was such a kind woman and her all-star staff was amazing, to say the least. They were some driven individuals who really loved their profession. They helped out patients, got them help, aid, support, held fundraisers and booths at a plethora of events. They spread the word about organ donation and transplantation.

Joining on as a volunteer was one of the best decisions of my life. I got to meet and bond with some outstanding transplant recipients such as, Amber Pettis (kidney), Patrick Johnson (kidney), Donald Hines (heart), Patrick Taylor (heart), Natalie Yates (kidney), Brian Lawson (lungs)...

Bobbie Betoni (heart) and Vera Johnson (heart).

I also got to meet donor mom Mrs. Barbara Edmond and a living kidney donor, Ms. Wanda Mason.

Not to mention the Rockstar staff that has become my extended family: Talisa Washington, Zola Burgess,

Randa Lipman, Michael Tate, Erskine Gillespie, Kassitee DeBardeleben, Yvonne Adams, Chris Franklin and many more.

These men and women have truly touched my life and honestly showed me what it was really like to be a blessing.

I was tremendously blessed to call each of these people my family and I looked forward to working alongside them…

And blessing others…

For many years to come.

CHAPTER 14:

BECOMING A LIVING TESTIMONY

Going through the volunteering program for the Mid-South Transplant Foundation had been a blessing and given me a platform to share my story within the foundation. Through my participation with the foundation, I was introduced to Donate Life's Transplant Games of America and featured in a documentary about my kidney journey and the road to my first transplant games.

The Donate Life Transplant Games was a multi-sport festival event produced by the Transplant Life Foundation for individuals who have undergone life-saving transplant surgeries.

Competition events were open to living donors, organ transplant recipients, bone marrow, corneal and tissue transplant recipients.

More than an athletic event, the Donate Life Transplant Games highlighted the critical importance of organ, eye, and tissue donation, while celebrating the lives of organ donors and recipients.

It was a dream come true to be able to participate in the Games.

I signed up for the 100, 200, and 400-meter dash in track and field. Being the son of athletes, my mom ran track and my dad played baseball in high school. I always dreamed of running track, but never got the chance to, due to kidney disease.

Now with the blessing of the Transplant Games of America, it gave us transplanted recipients the opportunity to be inclusive, to fulfill athletic dreams and also gave us a chance to win a metal.

So of course, I was going for the Gold. You didn't get too many opportunities where you got a shot at becoming a gold medalist. I wanted to give it everything I had.

For those who joined The Mid-South Transplant Foundation, they were now called #TeamMid-South.

The Foundation provided training for #Team Mid-South and those who were participating in the games.

Having a 6-month time span of training with Mr. Eric Shagard was a fun, yet challenging experience. I loved working out, however I only loved the cardio part. I hated lifting weights with a passion. I could run on the track, treadmill or bike all day, but as soon as Mr. Shagard had me go to the weights, I was ready to go.

Through the six months of training, I'd grown to "like" not love weightlifting. I was able to tolerate it a little more now.

He taught me form, technique and nutrition. I was loving the new-found energy and strength. I readied myself for the Transplant Games.

The 2016 games took place in Cleveland, Ohio. June 10th-15th.

I was 26 years old.

It was a life changing experience. To witness the many stories of other transplant journeys, the stories of donors and the support of their families tugged on my heart strings. It didn't leave a dry eye in the stadium during the opening ceremony.

Even though it was an Olympic-styled competition, it was mainly held to promote organ donation and transplantation.

My five days in Cleveland was fun, but when the day came for the track and field events, I was in serious mode.

I'd been training three days a week, for six months straight. This very moment empowered me.

It was a hot Saturday on the track of a local high school. My team and trainer were all there early to help cheer me on like they did for each team member.

Starting with the 400 meters, me and those in my age bracket ran the races. I was completely nervous, yet excited to hear the results, to see if I placed.

It was such a long wait. I began to humble myself, knowing I gave it my all. Whatever happened, happened.

If it was meant to be, it would be.

Long story short, I ended up placing third place in 400 meters at 14.21 seconds. I was shocked because I didn't think I would place in the race, but by the grace of God, I did.

I got to stand on the podium with the other winners. I was so proud and grateful for my moment that I got a little emotional. Even though it was only a bronze medal, I was thankful for that and treated it as if it was gold.

I still had the dream of being a gold medalist. I had to wait two years until the next games.

Time went by and the 2018 Transplant Games came around. I was 28 years old. This year it took place in Salt Lake City, Utah.

I participated in multiple events, such as the 5K Run/Walk, Soft ball toss, Discus, Bowling, Long jump and 4x100 meter relay, with three other team members.

Coming back to the Games, I was more determined. I had a better understanding of how the games operated.

I brought home a Gold and Silver medal.

I won the Gold medal in Long jump, jumping at 15.5 feet and the Silver medal, along with three of my #TeamMid-South teammates: Amber Pettis, Patrick Johnson and Patrick Taylor in a 4x100 meter relay.

I couldn't explain how thankful and proud of myself I was for me and the team. We'd all been working hard and the consistent support of each other over the past two years since the 2016 games was encouraging for all of us.

It was great to reign in victory, again, for the 2018 games. This year, #TeamMid-South brought home a record number of medals. We showed up and showed out!

We had a grand total of twenty medals. Everyone who participated in the games came back with a medal; some teammates came back with multiple medals.

After getting home from our big win in Utah, some of us did a bit of press, sharing the news. I personally did three radio shows and two live streams with a Kidney alliance organization.

I was completely on a high.

I was excited that the Lord blessed me to not only be a Gold Medalist, but also to trust me with giving my testimony about kidney disease; because He knew I would use my voice and experience to share it with the world on as many platforms as I could.

Living up to my promise the best way I knew how. I was honored to be one of the chosen ones. I was proud to say I endured. I persevered. Through the darkness, I was enlightened.

He decided to use me a vessel of inspiration, freedom, empowerment and education amongst those of the transplant community.

Sharing my personal journey from birth to transplantation and Becoming a Living Testimony was invigorating.

You, too, could have a successful life and live out your dreams.

With a great support system, determination, and faith, you'd be amazed on how God will use you and those around you.

Just pay attention to the signs…

God had a sense of humor when He wanted to get my attention.

So, pay attention…

And be obedient…

It'll take you a long way.

Trust me.

I AM A LIVING TESTIMONY!

I am living and breathing proof that the Lord could bless you in the midst of a storm.

He'd see you through, then bless you so you could live to bless other people.

Just hang in there, guys…

Your time is coming.

EPILOGUE:

160 BECOMING A LIVING TESTIMONY

I'd been asked a number of times what I meant by *Becoming a Living Testimony*? Well… One thing I'd learned over the years was, "There is a Blessing in transparency." Never would I be ashamed of the things I'd been through or overcame; so, every opportunity I got to be transparent, I didn't take it lightly. Exposing your truth could also be a testimony for someone else.

As for me and my life today, I was on a mission to inspire others along my journey and inspire those who battled kidney disease. I'd learned after the first ten years of transplant that I was continuously striving to be the person I wished I had to look up to as a teenager.

Someone who had been through dialysis, got a transplant and still pushed towards their dreams and goals.

Dialysis patients and recipients had been fed the negativity of kidney disease and how much of a hinderance it was to one's life. Yet, that might be true, but I believed it was all about how you looked at it. Perception.

Some people fed into it and some didn't. I honestly believed that kidney disease had indeed **BLESSED** my life and I outlined my journey in this book to prove it.

Now don't get me wrong, I'm not judging those who believe that kidney disease creates a hinderance to one's life—to each his own.

However, the way Gma Shirley raised me, she always encouraged me to think for myself and challenge everything I didn't 100% agree with.

I'd been told that some patients or recipients who underwent dialysis while in school either didn't finish or never excelled beyond a high school diploma. Not knocking those who didn't go to college because honestly, I didn't like school. The only reason I continued my education and received my master's degree was because in this day and age I felt like that was my only way out.

In addition to receiving my degree, I was also told that I shouldn't work. Folks had suggested that I should sit back and collect a Supplemental Security Income check (**SSI**) for the rest of my life.

I knew, early on, that that wasn't going to happen. I am not gonna lie, I lived off it until I got my bachelor's degree. And I was confident and secure enough to let it go once I began working, earning my own money.

I didn't want to become too dependent on a monthly check, to use it as a crutch and an excuse to not work, when I was well able to.

Again, I did understand that some people weren't able to do that. Some people were older or had other disabilities and just couldn't physically work.

Every patient was different. I was just speaking from my personal experiences.

I was fifteen when I received my kidney and I had big dreams. I refused to let **ANYBODY** tell me what I could and couldn't do. I, perhaps, couldn't do things like a regular person who wasn't on dialysis, or do things like someone who'd never dealt with kidney disease, but there's a way around everything.

It may take us a little longer, but it can be done.

I've been tremendously blessed in my career. I had the opportunity to share my story, talents and skills across many platforms.

When it came to my Artistic Vision, I've been blessed to work and collaborate creatively with some of the biggest organizations around the city of Memphis; such as the LeBonheur Children's Hospital, Methodist Hospital, Memphis Police Department, Memphis College of Art, Memphis Chamber of Commerce and Make-A-Wish Foundation, to name a few.

I became an entrepreneur and created my own campaign for artists called the **1 AM ART** Campaign. Sharing my passion for **ART** to make a difference and empowering the next generation of artists.

I've also had many opportunities to explore my dream of being an actor. As of now, I've starred in twenty-two stage plays, two documentaries and one short film.

I couldn't be more thankful for the doors that opened for me over the years and were still open to this day.

Being able to stay consistently focused on the promise I made with God and letting Him lead the way would always be my biggest testimony.

Having the ability to show other dialysis patients that no matter your disability, handicap, upbringing or hardships you can be anything you dream of. I'd been blessed to have supportive family and friends to carry me when my journey got tough and I felt like giving up.

It has been 16 years since I'd started my first dialysis treatment and this July 19th will be my 15-year kidney transplant anniversary…and on this very day of January 16, 2020, I am exactly 36 days away from my 30th birthday.

It'd been a long time coming, but I am a living witness.

No matter how long it take for you to reach your goals and dreams, if you keep going, you would eventually get there.

No matter the pace, just stay in the race. Your blessing and season is on its way.

I declare and decree that you would be tremendously blessed.
You won't be able to keep it to yourself.
Share your story with the world…
And help be a blessing to somebody else.

Take Care,
ARTavius Veasey

ACKNOWLEDGEMENTS

I will like to take this time to acknowledge and give thanks to a few special people and organizations whose played a big part in my life and becoming the man I am today.

Like the old saying goes, "It takes a village to raise a child," and I couldn't be more grateful of the village that took part in my growth to *Becoming A Living Testimony*.

First, I like to thank my father and living donor, Archie Veasey.

I could never repay you for this second chance at life that you've given me.

There are not enough thank you's in the world to show my appreciation for what you went through for this gift.

Thanks dad and I love you!

Secondly, my surgeon, Dr. Santiago Vera. Thank you for being the one who blessed my body with a successful transplant surgery.

I couldn't thank you enough sir.

Not for just my transplant surgery, but you were also my momma's surgeon for her kidney as well, so thank you from the bottom of my heart and may you continue to bless the bodies of other patients with successful transplant surgeries.

Thirdly, my pediatrician, Dr. Bettina H. Ault, MD.

I want to personally say thank you for being a part of my journey from birth all the way up to my transplant.

Thank you for never giving up on me and keeping me informed while educating me along the way.

I really appreciate and thank you for all you've done for me.

I will like to thank both LeBonheur Children's Hospital and The Med (Regional One Health) Hospital for taking good care of my dad and I during my dialysis treatments, hospital stays and our transplant surgery.

We really appreciated the hard work and dedication towards our care, and we couldn't thank you guys enough.

I will like to acknowledge my three superwomen of the Dialysis Unit at LeBonheur, Delores Evants, Violet Meyers and Sherry Wallace. You three have truly been a blessing sent from above.

The fun times and wisdom that each of you have shared with me has completely changed my mindset and I want to specifically say "Thank you" from the bottom of my heart.

I will like to acknowledge the amazing people of Camp Okawehna.

I'm beyond blessed for getting the opportunity to experience that week of what I referred to as stress therapy.

This camp has literally birthed the fighter that's within the person I am today.

Camp O is where I've learned to accept and believe in myself fully, no matter the situation nor circumstances I may be in.

I've learned that everything is temporary. If you stick within the fight of the storm it will be over before you know it.

It can't rain forever; the sun must eventually come out.

I pray that Camp O continues to grow and thrive for many more years to come.

Maybe even branch out or inspire other camps around the world.

I will like to give thanks to The Mid-South Transplant Foundation. You guys have been such a guiding light and resource, for not only me and my family, but for hundreds and thousands across the tri-state area.

Connecting patients with potential donors.

I can't thank y'all enough for all you do on and off the clock. I truly appreciate each of you.

I will like to acknowledge Donate Life's Transplant Games of America.

I can't explain how much love and respect I have for those who created such an historical and powerful event.

The stories and memories from this event alone are just untouchable from any other event of its kind.

I pray the legacy of this event continues for many more years and spreading awareness become more common and easier as time go on.

And last but certainly not least, I want to take this moment to give honor and acknowledgment to those who's passed on that has helped contribute to my journey towards transplantation and creating this book, Reginald (Reggie) Smith Jr., Tyler (King) Lane, Elizabeth (Ann) Barrett, Jerika Coleman and Jessica Louden.

I'm sorry y'all didn't get to witness the final product of the book.

I know y'all are here in spirit and watching over me, I hope I've made you proud.

I will forever cherish our memories as y'all now live through me. May your souls continue to rest in peace...

I love y'all.

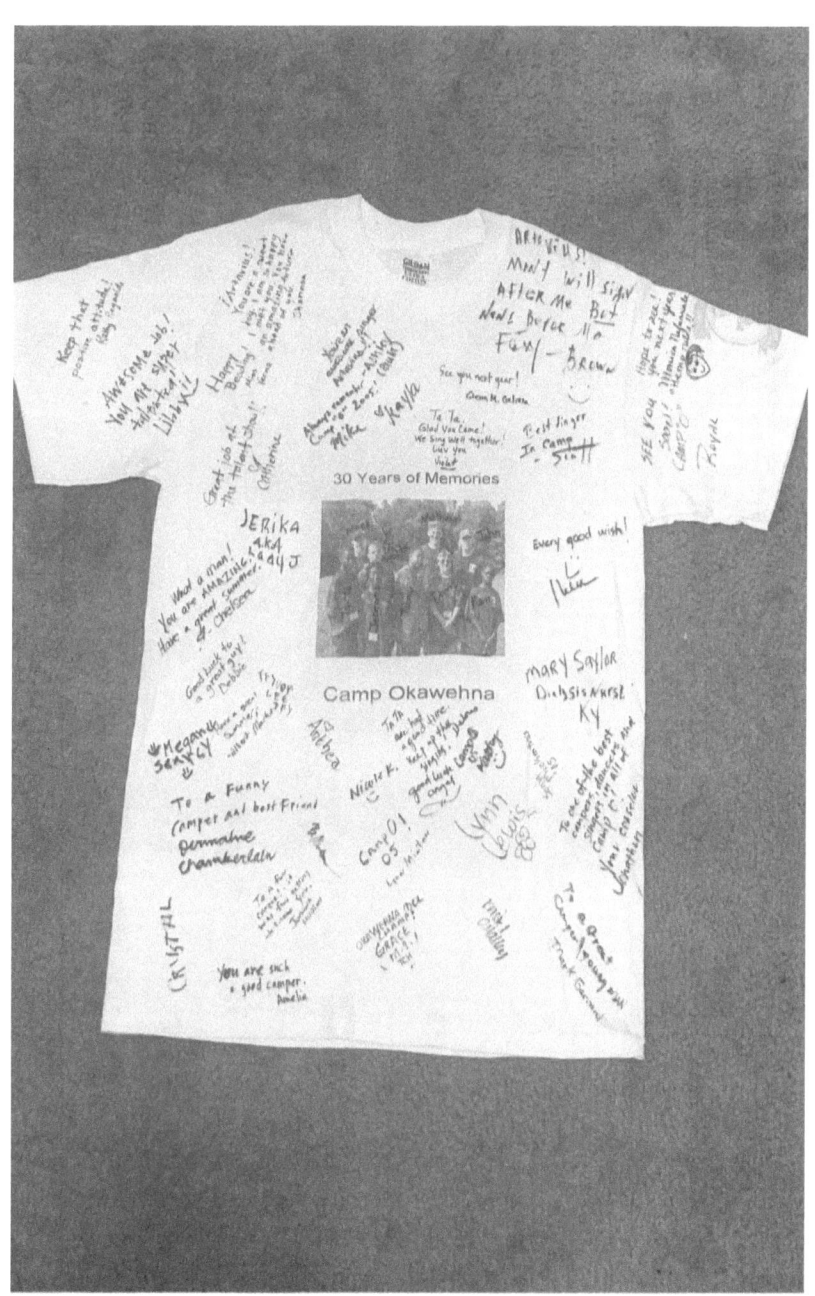

169 ARTavius Veasey

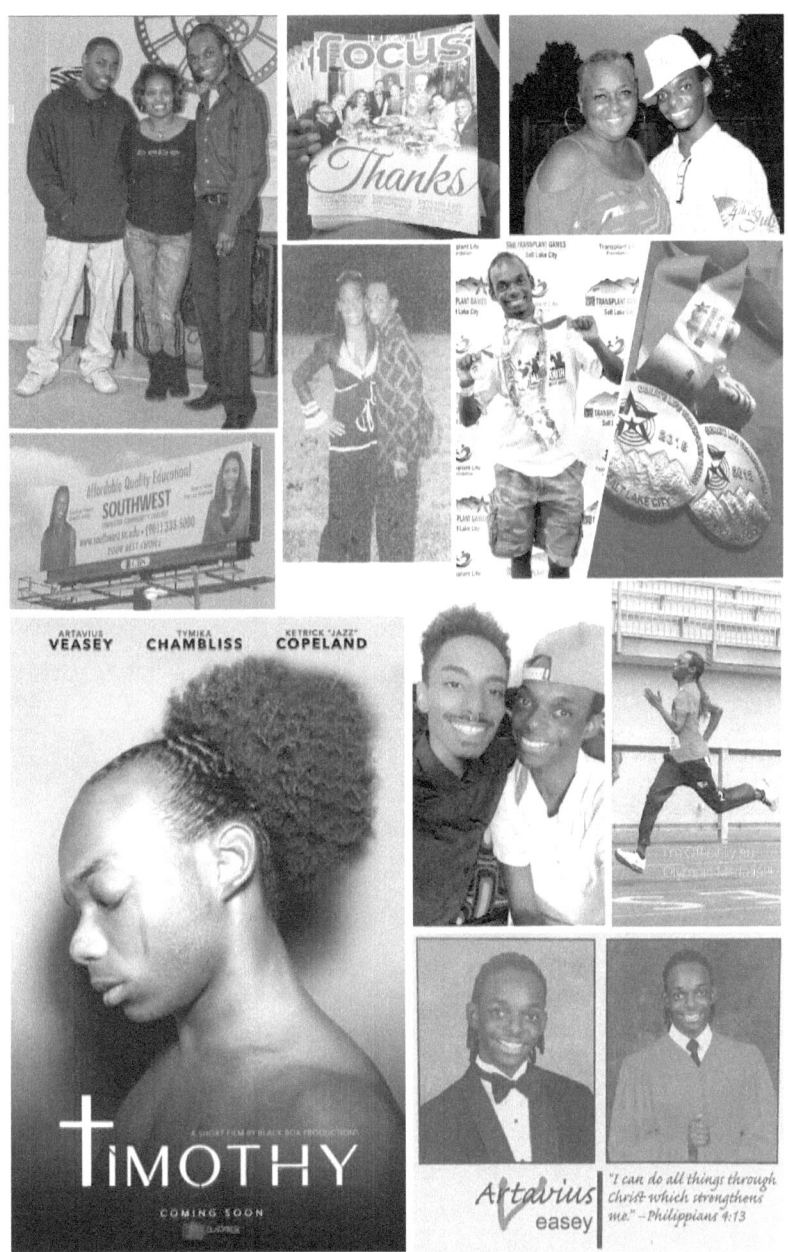

172 BECOMING A LIVING TESTIMONY

www.ingramcontent.com/pod-product-compliance
Lightning Source LLC
Chambersburg PA
CBHW021104080526
44587CB00010B/374